An A-Z of
HARRY POTTER

An A-Z of
HARRY POTTER

Everything You Always Wanted to Know
About The Boy Wizard and His Creator

Aubrey Malone

First published in Great Britain in 2007 by Friday Books

An imprint of The Friday Project Limited

83 Victoria Street, London SW1H 0HW

www.thefridayproject.co.uk

www.fridaybooks.co.uk

Text © Aubrey Malone 2007

ISBN 978-1-905548-97-2

British Library Cataloguing in Publication Data

A catalogue record for this book is available from the British Library

Cover design by Dignam Design and e-Digital Design

Internal design by e-Digital Design

Typeset by e-Digital Design

Printed by MPG Books Ltd

The Publisher's policy is to use paper manufactured from sustainable sources

Author's Note:

This is a selective guide to the *Harry Potter*
series and is not meant to be in any way
comprehensive. That would have taken a much
bigger book. But for those of you trying to jog
your memories about the seven books in the
series, it will hopefully fill a gap.

I have used the initials HP here and there
as shorthand for Harry Potter as a matter of
convenience. I have also shortened the titles of
the books for the same reason. Therefore,
Harry Potter and the Philosopher's Stone becomes
simply *The Philosopher's Stone*, and so on. All
words in bold have their own separate entries.

I would like to express my appreciation to all
the librarians who kindly directed me to
newspaper and magazine articles by and about
J K Rowling, on both sides of the Atlantic.

Sincere thanks to Clare Weber and The Friday Project

for taking on this book, and to Carrie Walker

and Miren Lopategui for their invaluable and

indispensable editing and proof reading.

Also to Des Duggan and Jim Stanley for instigating my

interest in the project, and to all the booksellers

who assisted me in my research.

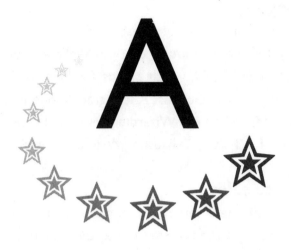

Abandonment

Many people imagine that J K Rowling was an overnight success because of her sudden explosion onto the literary scene. In some ways she was. Unlike most fledgling authors, she didn't wallpaper her room with rejection slips. But she did abandon two novels before hitting the jackpot with Harry Potter. What's the betting they won't turn up on some publisher's desk in the years to come? If so, she may well submit them under a pseudonym. Not using a pseudonym, she might feel, would give her an unfair advantage over the opposition.

Acronyms

Hermione coins one of these: 'SPEW', standing for 'Society, for the Promotion of Elfish Welfare'. Ron does likewise with 'SPUG', which stands for 'Society for the Protection of Ugly Goblins'. A less graphic one is 'OWL', shorthand for 'Ordinary Wizarding Level', and there's also 'NEWTS' for 'Nastily Exhausting Wizarding Tests'.

Advance sales

In July 2000, the internet site Amazon had clocked up advance sales of *The Goblet of Fire* to the tune of 290 000 copies. Two years later the VHS and DVD versions of *The Philosopher's Stone* were at the top of both the Amazon and Barnes & Noble websites as best-sellers three months before copies were actually available.

Age

Rowling turned 42 on 31 July 2007. She shares her birthday with – guess who – one Harry Potter.

Age line

This is the golden line Dumbledore drew around the Goblet of Fire to keep people under 17 years of age away from it. **Fred and George Weasley** took an Ageing Potion to try to circumvent it but they were still thrown back.

Alohamora

The spell Hermione uses to open the door in *The Philosopher's Stone* so she and her friends can escape without being caught out of bounds by **Argus Filch**.

Alternative career

Rowling was a teacher before she became a full-time writer. On her last day in the classroom she informed her class she was leaving the job. One bright spark piped up, 'Are you going to become a stripper, Miss?' Instead of telling him off she thanked him for the compliment.

Amnesty International

Rowling worked in this human rights organisation for a time, but left when she found that she was doing too much paperwork and not enough campaigning for causes. She worked secretly at her writing during lunch-breaks, which made her something of an oddity in the eyes of her colleagues. Was she having an affair, they wondered? In a sense she was – with her muse.

Anapneo

This term is Greek for 'breathe' and is said to the victim of a spell to reduce the ill effects of a blocked airway.

Animagus

This is a **wizard** ('magus' is Latin for wizard) who can transform him or herself into an animal. **Minerva McGonagall** turns herself into a cat at the beginning of the first book. **Sirius Black** becomes a dog – Harry mistakes him for a **Grim** – in *The Prisoner of Azkaban*, **Peter Pettigrew** transforms himself into a rat (with one of his toes missing because he himself is missing a finger), and even Harry's father, **James Potter**, became a stag at one point of his life, which led to his nickname of 'Prongs'.

Animagi reflect one's personality. Witness **Rita Skeeter** becoming a beetle. (Journalists are sometimes called deathwatch beetles because of their voyeuristic nature.) If Rowling could turn herself into an animal, she says she'd become an otter. (One might have expected her to say a **rabbit**, her favourite pet.) Hermione becomes one, reflecting this wish – Hermione being Rowling's alter ego in many ways.

Aparecium

This substance performs the unique feat of making invisible writing readable. Hermione used it to try to read **Tom Riddle**'s diary in *Chamber of Secrets* but it didn't work for her.

Apparate

Basically this means to appear. Its opposite, hardly surprisingly, is 'disapparate'.

Arachnophobia

A condition that Rowling – like Ron – suffers from. It means a fear of spiders.

Aragog

Giant spider-like creature with the gift of speech. It dies in *The Half-Blood Prince*.

Arantes, Jorge

Portuguese television journalist who married Rowling in 1992 when she'd gone to that country to teach. The marriage, however, lasted only little more than a year. In a violent outburst one night, he threw her out of their home after she told him she didn't love him any more. She stood on the street lost and forlorn, her whole world having crumbled... and her daughter **Jessica** unreachable inside with her fiery spouse. The police were called, a row ensued and Arantes finally parted from the little girl.

Rowling took Jessica back to **Edinburgh**, but Arantes followed her there. A period of intense friction followed. She finally obtained a restraining order against him and they formally divorced soon afterwards. He later wrote a kiss-and-tell article about her. Or perhaps that should be a write-and-tell one, because in it he claimed he had played a significant part in 'midwifing' Harry Potter. Rowling discounts this claim as arrant nonsense.

In one of the Potter books Rowling makes a wry reference to her wedding date, 16 October, by also making this the date Professor **Sibyll Trelawney** tells Lavender Brown a dreadful event will befall her. Hell hath no fury. It's also significant that Rowling wore black on her wedding day. Had she a Potter-like premonition that things would go wrong?

Arithmancy

Hermione's favourite subject, this is the process of predicting the future through numbers. It's also called numerology. It comes from two Greek words: 'arithmo' meaning number and 'mancy' meaning prophecy.

Arresto Momentum

This is the spell Dumbledore used to prevent Harry from falling to his death on the **Quidditch** pitch in *The Prisoner of Azkaban*.

Ascendio

Harry used this spell to rise up over the lake water in *Goblet of Fire*.

Aubrey, Bertram

A Hogwarts student from the 1970s. Harry's father once received detention for causing his head to double in size.

Auction

The first time Rowling heard her agent **Christopher Little** speaking to her about an auction she thought – furniture. Only later did it dawn on her that he was referring to a megabucks bidding war for her book. The rollercoaster ride had begun...

Austen, Jane

Rowling surprisingly lists this author as one of her main inspirations. She liked *Pride and Prejudice* as a teenager but her favourite Austen novel is *Emma*, which she claims to have read a whopping 20 times. From Austen's *Mansfield Park* she got the name of **Argus Filch**'s cat, **Mrs Norris**.

Autobiography

Rowling hasn't written this yet, but has spoken often about her life. The character who most resembles her in her books, she says, is Hermione. She admits she seemed to be something of a swot at school. (She read *Vanity Fair* at the tender age of 14!) Like Hermione, Rowling says she was insecure behind the perceived swot image. (However, she hasn't been known to cast spells with the same success as Ms Granger).

'I was neither as bright nor as annoying as Hermione,' she said in an interview once, adding that if she was she would have deserved 'drowning at birth'. She was, of course, only joking here. As the series goes on, Hermione becomes much less irksome when she realises there are more important things in life than reading and being first at exams – like friendship, for instance. (Rowling says she doesn't believe in magic either, except for the magic of love.)

Avada Kedavra

This is the curse that Voldemort used to kill Harry's parents (and almost Harry). It's Aramaic for 'abracadabra', which literally means 'Let the thing be destroyed'. (In its original usage it was a plea for a cure rather than a curse, the 'thing' being an illness.) Harry is the only person ever to have survived it, both at his birth and during a duelling bout with Voldemort wherein they both have similar **wands**, which detracts from their potential.

Azkaban

The prison from which **Sirius Black** escapes after turning himself into a dog. It sounds somewhat similar to Alcatraz, which was also high security and located on an island.

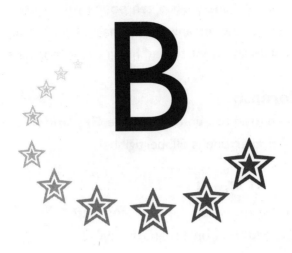

Babbling Beverage

Potion that causes the victim to talk nonsense. **Snape** threatens Harry with it in *The Order of the Phoenix*.

Bagshot, Bathilda

Author of *A History of Magic*, she was a family friend of the Dumbledores. She's killed by Voldemort in ***The Deathly Hallows***.

Baked beans

Rowling was so poor in her early writing career that one day when she tried to buy a tin of baked beans she found she was two pence short. To hide her embarrassment she pretended she'd left a ten pound note in her other coat. The beans, meanwhile, remained at the counter. Many nights she went to bed hungry before fame struck.

Balderdash

Password used to gain entry to the **Gryffindor** common room. Another one is Flibbertigibbet.

Balmoral Hotel

The venue at which Rowling completed *The Deathly Hallows* on 11 January 2007.

Banishing Charm

The opposite of the Summoning Charm.

Bans

In some countries Harry Potter books have been banned, thereby giving them even more publicity. Joking apart, the people who accuse them of encouraging children to practise witchcraft, or appearing to condone such an activity, are dramatically over-reacting to their subject matter. As Lisa Cherrett remarks in her book *The Triumph of Goodness* (published by the Bible Reading Fellowship), 'This immediately puts a barrier between Christian youngsters and their peers, and begins to breed in them the ghetto mentality of fear and suspicion.'

Banshee

A female spirit, derived from the Gaelic 'bean' (woman) and 'sí' (fairy), that wails and shrieks when death is imminent. No wonder Rowling's Irish character Seamus Finnigan (is there a nod to James Joyce's *Finnegans Wake here?*) is terrified by the prospect of them.

Interestingly enough, during Rowling's bohemian years, when she was drifting aimlessly between jobs and immersing herself in the dubious delights of punk rock, she formed an attachment to the music of a group called Síouxie and the Banshees, now long forgotten. This phase of her life was necessary for her to rid herself of her rebellious streak, paving the way for a time she would be entertained by the Queen – and end up out-earning her!

Bashu

Chinese publishing house that brought out three apocryphal Harry Potter novels, making quite a profit out of all of them before **Christopher Little**, Rowling's agent, put it out of business. The books were called *Harry Potter and the Leopard Walk up to Dragon*, *Harry Potter and the Golden Turtle* and *Harry Potter and the Crystal Vase*.

Basilisk

The terrifying serpent in *Chamber of Secrets* that can turn people to stone. The only thing that can control a Basilisk is a **Parselmouth**. One of them killed **Moaning Myrtle**.

Bell, Katie

One of the three **Chasers** on the **Gryffindor Quidditch** team.

Bibliomania

Rowling is so fond of reading she says that if she finds herself in a bathroom with no books, she reads the labels on the toiletries.

Bildungsroman

A novel dealing with the spiritual, moral, psychological and social development of its main character, from the above German term that translates directly as 'novel of education'. The Harry Potter saga certainly fits this particular bill.

Binns, Professor

This is Harry's History of Magic professor. We can see what Harry and/or Rowling think of his ability by dint of his surname, though when Hermione asks him about the Chamber of Secrets in the book of that name, all the class are agog. Unfortunately, in the American version of the book, 'dustbin' is changed to 'trash can' so this pun is lost. Binns, it should be added, is a ghost, having forgotten to bring his body to class with him one day. (As you would.) He enters the classroom through the blackboard.

Birthdays
Harry was born on the same date as Rowling: 31 July. **Daniel Radcliffe**, who plays him in the films, was also born in July, though not 31 July, as Connie Ann Kirk mistakenly states in her biography of Rowling.

Black, Regulus
Younger brother of Sirius.

Black, Sirius
The literal meaning of his name is 'Black Dog'. He's Harry's godfather and the former best friend of Harry's father, but we initially fear him after he escapes from **Azkaban** because we hear he's a serial killer. Only later does it emerge that he's been framed by **Peter Pettigrew** and is actually on Harry's side. (Unfortunately, he dies before managing to clear his name.) He's also his secret benefactor, providing him with his trusty Firebolt broomstick. Black dies protecting Harry from Voldemort, which is a pity as he was a popular character with readers, and one of Harry's few true allies.

Blood

Wizards can be pure-bloods or half-bloods. **Draco Malfoy** is a pure-blood (this in fact being his password to get into the **Slytherin** common room) whereas **Tom Riddle** and Harry himself are half-bloods. Those born of **Muggle** parents are 'filthy little Mudbloods', as Malfoy delights in reminding them. When Hermione reaches higher academic standards than he does, he puts it down to teacher favouritism. Rowling has ostensibly written a wizard story but the class struggle is ubiquitous. The fact that she makes the aristocratic pure-blood the villain nails her democratic colours to the mast very early on. Her background in the classics has enabled her to capture the collegiate atmosphere to a 't', but she's also known poverty and has an empathy with the poor, like Ron and his siblings. Her books undermine elitism from the inside.

Bloody Baron

The house ghost of **Slytherin**.

Bloomsbury

Rowling's publishers, who offered her an advance of £2000 for her first book in 1996. It was a huge amount to her at that time as her marriage had just broken down and she was living on lean rations, but of course it would be mere pocket money to her now.

Bludgers

The balls used in **Quidditch** that try to knock players off their broomsticks.

Blyton, Enid

People sometimes denigrate Rowling by saying her books are little more than Enid Blyton on broomsticks. She says herself that she was never really a fan of that author, though she's read the Famous Five books, and certain elements of the solidarity of Harry, Ron and Hermione are similar as they go about their fact-finding missions and suddenly end up in life-threatening situations before all comes out well in the end.

The difference, of course, is that there's a Peter Pan element with the Famous Five. They remain the same age throughout all the books, unlike Rowling's characters, who go through hormonal changes in adolescence, like 'real' children. Rowling originally intended to bring out one book a year but interruptions of one sort or another gave rise to delays; this has affected the timescale of the films as well, which means that her characters have aged more quickly on the screen than in the books.

Boarding schools

Rowling seems to celebrate these in her books, but says she's not exactly a fan of them. (She never went to one, and nor did **Enid Blyton**, another author who liked writing about them.) Rowling's critics say this element of her work makes it a thinly disguised lament for ye olde England, but that hasn't stopped readers lapping it up, even (especially?) if it has a certain anachronistic element.

Even though Harry is a **wizard**, he has to worry about things like homework, exams, practical jokes, teasing, detention, boring classes (**Professor Binns** take a bow!), one-upmanship, punctuality, peer group pressure, not wandering out of bounds, succeeding at games, etc. Rowling weaves these details seamlessly into all the chapters dealing with spells, potions, trolls, owl posts, **centaurs**, **boggarts**, sphinxes, **Basilisks**, werewolves, secret passageways, passwords, flying broomsticks, death curses, giant spiders, speaking snakes and so on.

Hogwarts is a co-ed, multicultural school of learning with Head Girls, Head Boys and prefects. It doesn't have flogging, like, say, the institutions of the *Tom Brown's School Days* era of literature – point deduction is the preferred mode of censure – nor does it have 'fagging', i.e. the practice of new pupils becoming older ones' gofers, though the house elves seem to some extent to serve this function. Like Tom Brown, however, Harry is bullied, he's good at sports, he breaks rules when he feels he has to, he has a wise headmaster – Brown's was Dr Arnold while his is Professor Dumbledore – and he eventually becomes a hero to his class.

What Rowling has done is to serve up old wine in new wineskins, as well as throwing in some occult villainy for good (or bad) measure, and we relish the unique mix.

Boggarts

These chameleon-like creatures can take the form of any-thing they wish, depending on what the person looking at them is fearing. Rowling probably based the word on the bogeyman. You can get the better of them by imagining diverse things at once and making them assume shapes one finds amusing.

Book signings

Rowling's have been compared to *Rolling* (Rowling?) *Stones* concerts for their hysteria and hype. At one in Boston in 1999, she signed no less than 1400 books in a single day. She must have wished for a magic signature **wand** that day to stave off a stinging wrist.

Borgin & Burkes

Shop on **Knockturn Alley** where one can buy items relating to the **Dark Arts**.

Branagh, Kenneth

The actor who plays the sensationally narcissistic **Gilderoy Lockhart**… with sensational narcissism.

Bryce, Frank

The caretaker of Riddle House.

Bubble-Head Charm

A spell that encloses the caster in a bubble of air. **Cedric Diggory** uses it to travel underwater without drowning in *The Goblet of Fire*.

Buckbeak

This is the **hippogriff** that **Hagrid** brings to his Care of Magical Creatures class. Harry approaches him gently, winning his confidence and succeeding in flying him. **Draco Malfoy**, however, annoys him and Buckbeak slashes his arm. Malfoy exaggerates the injury and Buckbeak is sentenced to death. Hermione rescues him posthumously with her trusty **Time-Turner**, and **Sirius Black** rides away on him, thereby sparing both of their lives.

Budleigh Babberton

The village where **Horace Slughorn** lives as a recluse before Dumbledore prevails upon him to return to Hogwarts.

Burnings

It's hard to believe that reactions to Rowling's work would be so emotive that her books would actually be burned by those who felt they exercised unhealthy influences on impressionable children, but this is exactly what happened in New Mexico in 2001 when Jack Brock, a pastor of the Alamogordo Community Church, organised a communal burning of the texts, his congregation singing 'Amazing Grace' as the volumes went up in flames. Another burning took place in Pennsylvania around about the same time. Ironically, such incidents only increased Rowling's cult status. (Banning of books often has the same effect.)

C

Caine, Michael

Rowling's favourite actor.

Camp-outs

Activities performed by diligent fans of Harry Potter, who sometimes queue late at night to be first in line for the latest title to appear on the shelves at midnight. The 'witching hour' would seem to be an appropriate time to sell books about witches.

Carroll, Lewis

Another major influence on Rowling, particularly if we liken her work to the 'beautiful nonsense' of *Alice in Wonderland*.

Like Carroll, Edward Lear, Dr Seuss and others, Rowling likes the idea of mirrors leading to magic portals.

Carrow, Alecto
The **Death Eater** who invaded Hogwarts in 1997 with her brother Amycus.

Cassettes
Over a million cassettes and CD recordings of Harry Potter books have been sold at the time of writing.

Censorship
In some states in the US, Rowling's books have been withdrawn from school libraries because they're deemed to romanticise the gothic and condone occultism. Some of her denouncers have even accused her of being responsible for children browsing the net in search of Satanic cults. A lady called Carol Rockwood, the head teacher at a Church of England Primary School in Chatham, Kent, also banished Rowling's books from her library in 2000 because she believed that the 'devils, demons and witches are real and pose the same threat as, say, a child molester'. There's even 'The Organisation of People Against Potter' (TOOPAP), and in Austria a Harry Potter 'hate line' where critics work through their grievances by phone.

Rowling's own view is that we should censor the censors, not the books, which she sees as innocuous and therapeutic. She has never, she claims, met a child who wanted to be a witch or wizard after reading anything she wrote. 'People find anything in a book if they wish,' she claims.

The Christian overtones of the books can also be seen in details like the children going home from Hogwarts for Christmas and Easter holidays, though such matters are handled in secular fashion. The snake symbol of the evil **Slytherin** House is also a Christian one. In much the same way as **J R R Tolkien** and **C S Lewis** incorporated Christian concepts into fantasy literature, Rowling also has this subtext. Her work is really about moral choices, the ones we all face as we try to negotiate our way through grey areas. The fact that these issues are couched in mythical contexts does nothing to detract from their didactic nature.

What Rowling is basically saying is that we can be masters of our destiny even against apparently insuperable odds. If we think about **boggarts**, or the Mirror of **Erised**, what they share in common, despite superficial differences, is that we can influence what we see in the mirror, or what shape the boggart takes on. One encapsulates our desires and the other our fears. To this extent, they're corollaries of each other. Harry learns to assert himself over his fate, and to this extent the books are actually old-fashioned. As Edmund Kern writes in *The Wisdom of Harry Potter* (Prometheus Books), 'If children reading the books grow up to be greedy consumers, intolerant chauvinists or dabblers in malevolent witchcraft, they will not do so because of what they read in Harry's adventures.'

Neither does the violence in the novels lead to violence in the real world because it's so obviously fantasy-driven. In the main what Rowling is writing are so many allegories of the primeval battle between good and evil.

In North Carolina some years ago, however, a young girl jumped off a kitchen table with a broomstick, imagining she would be able to fly after reading *The Philosopher's Stone*. She wasn't seriously injured but critics of Rowling use anecdotes like these as sticks to beat her with. Pursuing such an analogy would lead to calls to ban *Superman* comics for fear their readers would try to jump off buildings and fly as a result, or calls to censor **C S Lewis'** *Chronicles of Narnia* because they feature astrology. Rowling has emphasised that her ambition was to make wizardry not fearful, but fun. She wanted to demythologise and domesticate an erstwhile eerie genre. She has, in effect, created Harry in Wonderland.

Her books encourage noble behaviour, and if Harry occasionally breaks rules or tells lies, that's no reason to undermine Rowling's overall ambition. She's merely trying to make him into a three-dimensional character. Everyone, from Huckleberry Finn to Holden Caulfield, the narrator of *The Catcher in the Rye*, has in their way shunned convention to find their identity. Rowling isn't condoning rebellion. She's merely telling us we shouldn't be sheep – especially if we live in a spider-infested **cupboard** at Number 4, **Privet Drive**.

Centaurs

These creatures, which are half man and half horse, appear in *The Philosopher's Stone* as friends of Hagrid. Their names are Ronan and Bane. See also **Firenze**.

Chang, Cho

Harry develops a crush on this pretty **Seeker** for the **Ravenclaw Quidditch** team and as a result asks her to accompany him to the Yule Ball – though she turns him down for **Cedric Diggory**, foolish lass. After Diggory is killed she and Harry become an item, as they say, but Cho is threatened by the presence of Hermione. Cho gives Harry his first kiss in *Order of the Phoenix*. She's an exotic character to be sure, but rather sketchily drawn and not too significant in the overall scheme of things.

Charities

Rowling is a generous patron of Edinburgh's Maggie's Centre, which helps cancer sufferers, as well as the National Council for One Parent Families, and the Multiple Sclerosis Society of Scotland. She's never suffered from cancer but a close friend of hers did. Her mother died from multiple sclerosis, which devastated her, and she's also a single mother, having had a child with **Jorge Arantes**.

Chasers

There are three of these on a **Quidditch** team. Harry's father **James Potter** was one. Ability at this game clearly ran in the Potter family.

Children

Rowling says she prefers children rather than adults to interview her at book signings. They ask better questions, she believes. Who better to understand a child than a child?

Children's author

The stand-up comedian Steven Wright tells this joke: 'I wrote a few children's books – not on purpose.' For too long this genre has been the Cinderella of literature. In the same sense as children were once looked on as unformed adults, so children's writing has inhabited a kind of limbo for authors who are perceived to be unsuccessful (or, as Mr Wright would have it, accidental) 'adult' writers. Rowling dislikes being called a children's author as she feels her books can be equally appreciated by adults. An enormous number of adults agree. As Elizabeth Heilman writes in *Harry Potter's World* (Routledge), as far back as 1998 adults were reading them 'behind false grown-up covers' to hide their secret addictions. (They've since come out of the closet because the books are now published in adult editions as well as children's ones.)

'I never saw myself as consciously writing for children,' Rowling claims, 'but rather for myself.' She adds that she doesn't feel she has to write a quote unquote adult book to earn herself bona fide authorial chops. However, one gets the impression she has a sneaking wish to write a book (or many books) for adults in the future. Adult writers she admires are Nabokov and Roddy Doyle – particularly for *Lolita* and *The Woman Who Walked Into Doors*, respectively. The latter book has marital disharmony as its theme – something Rowling can well identify with. Doyle has also written evocatively about childhood, especially in his Booker Prize-winning novel, *Paddy Clarke Ha Ha Ha*.

Chipping Sodbury

Rowling was born in a village called Yate, close to Chipping

Sodbury. The latter sounds much more exotic than Yate, so she generally tells interviewers it was here she came into the world. It was, she says, 'a place that doomed me to a love of weird place names'.

Chocolate frogs

These delicacies are the delight of Hogwarts students, and carry the added attraction of coming with cards. Rowling says she likes food to be identified in books in great detail, and that's exactly what she does herself with her endless inventories of goodies such as Jelly Slugs, Fizzing Whizbees, Bertie Bott's Every Flavour Beans, etc. (One of her favourite authors, **Elizabeth Goudge**, featured food significantly in her book *The Little White Horse*). The idea of the cards forms an easy identification with children who would buy certain items to collect cards featuring movie stars, soccer players, etc.

Cinderella

Rowling is often portrayed as a Cinderella figure, a kind of female Harry who lived, if not in a **cupboard**, at least in very reduced circumstances. This has caused many myths to grow up about her pre-fame days, some of which are rather humorous. One story alleged that she wrote her first book on table napkins, as if she was unable to afford a notepad. 'The next thing', she joked, 'they'll be telling me I wrote it on used tea bags.'

Cleese, John

Cleese does an idiosyncratic turn as **Nearly Headless Nick** in *The Philosopher's Stone*. (So what else is new?) Rowling is an avid fan of the Monty Python series in general and Cleese in particular. She greatly enjoyed the dizzy lunacy he brought to the role of Nick.

Coffee

Endless cups of espresso gave Rowling the adrenalin to continue pushing her pen across the page when she was drained from mothering duties. She often talks about her days trying to manoeuvre **Jessica**'s buggy down the stairs of **Nicolson's** café in **Edinburgh**, her knees trembling from the caffeine fix.

Colloportus

Hermione uses this spell to seal a door when she's trying to stop the **Death Eaters** from escaping after they grab Harry.

Coltrane, Robbie

This genial Scot, best known for his role in television's *Cracker*, plays **Hagrid** in the film versions of the Harry

Potter books. The special effects department obviously worked overtime to make him look Hagrid's size but he's hardly wasting away anyway, even without the camera tricks. One of his problems with car seatbelts, he says, is trying to get the lap strap on! He has expressed a wish to join Overeaters Anonymous. He wants to be able to call a counsellor whenever he feels peckish so that he can be talked out of it.

Columbus, Christopher

The director with the same name as the man who discovered America made the first two Harry Potter movies. Rowling appreciated how he handled child star Macaulay Culkin in *Home Alone*. He also made *Mrs Doubtfire* with Robin Williams and worked as a screenwriter on children's films such as *Gremlins*, *The Goonies* and *Young Sherlock Holmes*.

Comic Relief

Rowling took time out from the Potter series to pen two books for this charity, both published in 2001. They've raked in over £20 million to date. They're called *Quidditch Through the Ages* and *Fantastic Beasts and Where to Find Them*. The former comes with a glowing Foreword from the redoubtable Professor Dumbledore, who cites it as one of the most popular titles in Hogwarts library. Rowling has fun with the book, but on the back page reminds us that the charity she's supporting is 'even more important and astonishing than the three and a half second capture of the Golden Snitch by Roderick Plumpton in 1921'. Indeed. The US edition is priced in Sickles and Knuts.

Confidentiality

Rowling guards her plots with fierce privacy for obvious reasons. When she gave the completed text of *The Philosopher's Stone* to **Christopher Columbus**, who was about to direct the movie version, he wasn't even allowed to show it to his children. After Rowling's seventh and last Harry Potter outing had been completed, the text was kept under lock and key in a vault as secure as **Vault 713** at **Gringotts** Bank.

Conjunctivitis Curse

A spell that affects the eyes of the victim.
Viktor Krum uses it in *The Goblet of Fire*.

Connery, Sean

The James Bond star was originally offered the role of Dumbledore. He declined, and **Richard Harris** stepped in.

Corner, Michael

Cho Chang's boyfriend.

Counselling

Waterstone's children's manager Wayne Winstone said, after the publication of **The Deathly Hallows**, 'This could be a similar moment to when Take That split up – there could be a lot of upset teenagers out there. We're looking at setting up a helpline for them.'

Crabbe, Vincent

Draco Malfoy's rather dim bodyguard, alongside **Gregory Goyle**, who seems only slightly less dim. (The terms Goyle – reminding one of 'gargoyle' – and Crabbe speak for themselves.) Both have more brawn than brains and use each other as crutches. Like most bullies, including Draco, they're probably lily-livered at heart. They accompany Draco everywhere like extensions of his body, providing moral (or should that be immoral) support for him in his endless taunting of Ron and Harry.

Critics

No author pleases everyone. The movie critic Leslie Halliwell wrote of The Philosopher's Stone: 'A curious mish-mash of fairytale, myth, fantasy and British public school ritual. All that seems to be missing, regretfully, is Billy Bunter and the girls from St. Trinian's.' He added grudgingly, 'Some splendid production designs add visual interest to the bland proceedings.' Rowling, no doubt, cried her way to the bank.

Crookshanks

Hermione's cat, who warns her that Scabbers isn't all he seems.

Crouch, Barty

A **wizard** who, like Voldemort, kills his father. Crouch Senior, his namesake, sent him to **Azkaban** after he got into trouble with the Ministry of Magic.

Cruciatus Curse

The one used by **Bellatrix Lestrange** to drive **Neville Longbottom**'s parents insane. Its incantation is 'Crucio' and it's one of the **Unforgivable Curses**.

Cuarón, Alfonso

The director of *Harry Potter and the Prisoner of Azkaban*. He also makes a cameo appearance in the movie, playing a **wizard** in the **Leaky Cauldron** shop. The direction of the film was beset with problems, including a worker's strike and a train crash on the set that caused a fire, resulting in the destruction of 100 acres of heathland.

Cuffe, Barnabus

Editor of the **Daily Prophet**.

Cupboard

The fact that Harry is forced to live in a cupboard under the stairs by his cruel step-parents may be a metaphor for the fact that there's a skeleton in that cupboard – the secret of his parents' death at the hands of Voldemort rather than in a car accident, as Vernon **Dursley** insists.

Curtis, Jamie Lee

This actress (the daughter of Tony) was the first to suggest to **Daniel Radcliffe**'s mother that he would be a good choice for Harry on screen.

Cushioning Charm

This makes flying by broomstick less arduous by creating an invisible 'pillow' on the stick.

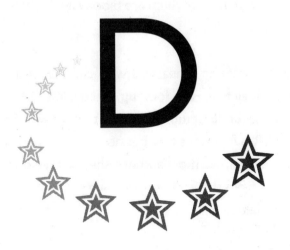

Dahl, Roald

Dahl is probably one of the strongest influences on Rowling, from the point of view of both style and character, though she herself thinks she's a much more realistic writer than he is and isn't a fan of his. Nonetheless, Harry's childhood is similar in many ways to events in Dahl's *James and the Giant Peach*. James (whose surname is Trotter, not Potter) has evil guardians like the **Dursley family** and shares many personality traits with Harry. Another novel by Dahl, *Matilda*, featured a young girl whose bullying parents kept calling her stupid even though she was much smarter than they were. Dahl once said, 'There are 40 000 children's books printed in Britain every year, and most of them are bloody awful, pulped, and never reprinted.'

He believed that to empathise with children you had to go down on all fours and look up at the adults. This would help one to understand their point of view – literally. Like Dahl, Rowling does this. But her voice is unmistakably her own, even if, like most authors, she's soaked up moods and images from the voracious reading she's been engaged in all her life.

Daily Prophet

The most popular **wizard** publication in Potterworld.

Dark Arts, The

Black magic. Professors of Defence Against the Dark Arts at Hogwarts have a rather hapless time, the position being something of a poisoned chalice.

Dark Mark

What the **Death Eaters** have burned into their arms as a sign of allegiance to Voldemort. It also acts as a form of communication from Voldemort and appears when they've killed someone.

Death Eaters

Disciples of Voldemort who help him back to strength after the spell he casts on Harry rebounds on him. After his downfall they claim they acted against their will. If we wish to pursue a Nazi analogy (see **Durmstrang**) we will remember many of Hitler's high-ranking disciples did likewise at their trials after World War 2.

Deathday party

Nearly Headless Nick organises this. What else would a ghost have – especially if he's 500 years old?

Deathly Hallows, The

In the context of Rowling's final book, the eponymous terms refer to items bequeathed by Death to three **wizards** who cheated death. These are an **Elder Wand**, a Resurrection Stone and an **Invisibility Cloak**.

Rowling says this is her favourite of all the books and also the one that was most difficult to write. She confessed to Jonathan Ross in an interview that she gushed tears after killing off one of her 'big' characters in it. (Although she didn't say which one.)

Such was the secrecy surrounding the book that it was rumoured to have been printed in the dark at

Bloomsbury to stop printers having a peek at its contents. It was launched at 12.01 a.m. on 21 July 2007 in bookshops everywhere. Many shops organised extravagant displays for the occasion and had theme parties. Some fans were so anxious to find out what happened to the characters that they read their book throughout the night and finished it by dawn.

Every bookshop signed an embargo clause stipulating that none of the boxes of books would be opened until the appointed hour. No cameras were allowed into shops for fear of pages being photographed. Some chapters were leaked on a US internet site, and **Scholastic** threatened legal action as a result. Scholastic printed an unprecedented 12 million copies for its first run. The book takes Rowling's overall page count to an awe-inspiring 3419 pages, or 1.4 million words.

Dedication

Rowling dedicated her first book to her mother, her sister and her daughter. Her father's name was conspicuously absent. This was probably indicative of a rift in their relationship. (Her mother hadn't even been dead for two years when he remarried.) This rift has been healed for some years now.

Delacour, Fleur

A rather snooty Veela whose name literally means 'flower of the court'. She marries Bill Weasley in *The Deathly Hallows*.

Deletrius

The spell Amos Diggory uses to get rid of the ghost image of the **Dark Mark** in *Goblet of Fire*.

Deluminator

A gadget that puts out lights. Dumbledore leaves one to Ron in his will. It's also called a **Put-Outer**.

Dementors

These horrific soul-sucking creatures in *The Prisoner of Azkaban* are guardians of that prison and later of Hogwarts. They've been aptly described as 'soul vampires'. Rowling said she saw them as forms of depression, a condition she herself suffered from at one time of her life when she was poor, divorced and trying to come to terms with the early death of her mother. They drain happiness from whoever comes into contact with them. The word 'dementor' is similar to 'dementia' and also reminds us of the expression 'You have me demented.' Chocolate lifts one's spirits after coming into contact with them, as happens when Professor **Lupin** gives Harry chocolate to warm him on the train when he succumbs to his first Dementor attack. (Chocolate also seems to lift the spirits of depressed humans.)

Densuageo

A spell that gives buck teeth to its victim. **Draco Malfoy** uses it in *Goblet of Fire*, meaning it for Harry but inflicting it on Hermione instead.

Dervish & Bangs

A **wizard** equipment shop in **Hogsmeade**.

Derwent, Dilys

This character was a healer at **St Mungo's** from 1722 to 1741 and thereafter a headmistress at Hogwarts. Her portrait hangs in Dumbledore's office.

Desert islands

Rowling was asked who she would least like to be with on a desert island. Surprisingly, she didn't choose Voldemort. 'Voldemort would not be good in the sense that he would kill me,' she admitted – an important consideration! – 'but I would rather die than be stuck with **Gilderoy Lockhart** or **Dolores Umbridge**.' Them's fightin' words where I come from.

Diagon Alley

This cobbled street which leads to **Gringotts** is shaped 'diagonally', so Rowling is making a clever pun.

Dickens, Charles

As with Dickens, the eccentric names of Rowling's characters – **Cedric Diggory**, **Gilderoy Lockhart**, etc. – give us an insight into their characters. Dickens would also have had an empathy with Rowling's creation of an orphaned child with a mysterious past who's constantly mistreated by his foster parents.

Diffindo

A spell that's used to cut something open.

Diggory, Cedric

Hufflepuff's **Quidditch** captain who's killed by Voldemort in *The Goblet of Fire*. His death is Harry's first real exposure to evil at first hand, the murder of his parents having happened when he was too young to be a witness in any concrete sense.

Dinky Diddydums

Petunia **Dursley**'s pet name for her son Dudley. Another equally cloying one is 'Ickle Diddykins'.

Divination

The art of seeing into the future by means of the stars, crystal balls or tea leaves.

Dobby

The house elf who does his best to discourage Harry from returning to Hogwarts for his second year. He was originally owned by the Malfoys but turned against them to help Harry and then became racked with guilt. He was released from servitude to them by a trick Harry used involving an old sock. (Contact with an owner's clothing frees an elf.) Harry always showed kindness to him and Dobby responded to this, but he was subsequently torn in his loyalties, which leads to cries of 'Bad Dobby!' as he beats himself up.

After Dobby was freed from the Malfoys he went to work in the Hogwarts kitchen because he became bored with his freedom. But at least here he has a master he likes: Dumbledore. Dumbledore tells Dobby he can call him 'a barmy old codger' if he wishes, something that would have been unthinkable for the Malfoys.

Afterwards he teams up with **Kreacher** to spy on **Draco Malfoy**. He always speaks of himself in the third person.

Sadly, **Bellatrix Lestrange** knifes him to death in *The Deathly Hallows*.

Doge, Elphias

The writer of Dumbledore's obituary.

Dolohov, Antonin

One of the five **Death Eaters** who murdered **Gideon and Fabian Prewett**. He's killed by **Professor Flitwick** in the Second Battle of Hogwarts towards the end of *The Deathly Hallows*.

Doniger, Wendy

Critic who said Rowling's best talent was for absorbing elements from different types of fiction in a process she called 'bricolage'. According to Doniger, Rowling's books are little more than thinly disguised melanges of *Peter Pan*, *Snow White* and *Mary Poppins*.

Dual identity

Many characters in fantasy have double lives. Clark Kent became Superman, Peter Parker became Spiderman, etc. Harry lives a subdued life in the **cupboard** under the stairs at the **Dursleys**' and appears timid like Kent and Parker, but of course he shows his superhuman powers when he goes to Hogwarts.

Dumbledore, Aberforth and Ariana

Albus' brother and sister respectively.

Dumbledore, Albus

This authoritative character, Hogwarts' chief **wizard**, is the nemesis of Voldemort, Rowling's Prince of Darkness, so it's apt that 'albus' means 'white'. 'Dumbledore' is more obscure, being an old English term for bumblebee. Rowling said she imagined him humming to himself, which is why she chose the name. Such a quality suggests that he's very much at ease with himself and with life, as indeed he is. He even speaks about death as being 'but the next great adventure'. Significantly, Sir James Barrie, whom Rowling resembles in many ways, has his most famous character Peter Pan speaking of death as 'an awfully big adventure'. Two films based on the staging of *Peter Pan* also carry this title.

Dumbledore seems like an omniscient, even God-like figure in the books, He speaks enigmatically to Harry as if he's always one step ahead of him in his quest for information, feeding him snippets like clues to some abstruse jigsaw as he grooms him for greatness. (Significantly, only he and Harry refer to Voldemort by name.) He speaks in teasing epigrams, a bit like Rowling herself in interviews, hinting at what he hides as he advises Harry not to be too inquisitive, that all will be explained in time.

It's our choices that define us, he states, rather than our abilities. Elsewhere he says it's not what we're born as that matters, but what we become. These may appear to be clichés, but clichés are often true. The point about Dumbledore is that he doesn't impose his wisdom on Harry. He knows that, as the poet W B Yeats once said, 'We cannot know truth; we can only embody it.' In the same way, Dumbledore knows that one day Harry will under-stand the meaning of all his sayings, and their relevance to him. In the meantime the only way it seems Harry will ever really know what's going on in Dumbledore's mind, we feel, is if he gets inside it, which he does of course when he goes into his **Pensieve**.

Some commentators feel that Dumbledore is partly modelled on Merlin from the King Arthur legend, or **Tolkien**'s Gandalf. He's a kindly patriarchal figure who seems to be Harry's best chance against Voldemort... until he's sensationally killed off in Book Six at the age of 150. The deaths of other 'big' characters like **Cedric Diggory** and **Sirius Black** now somehow recede into the background. Harry, however, meets Dumbledore again in a spiritual state in *The Deathly Hallows*.

Durmstrang

This is the institute of wizardry presided over by **Igor Karkaroff**. It gets its name from the German phrase 'sturm und drang' which means 'storm and stress'. Dumbledore defeated the evil **wizard** Grindelwald in 1945, the year World War 2 ended, so there's another German connection here. Durmstrang doesn't admit Mudbloods so we can see a third connection to the Nazi idea of the master race in such segregation, which has undertones of ethnic cleansing. In the book *Re-Reading Harry Potter* (Palgrave Macmillan), author Suman Gupta writes: 'The alignment of absolute evil that is Voldemort and the Dark Side has the fascist desire for pure-blood as its ideological characteristic, and master-servant bonding as its organisational mode.' This also brings us into the whole area of the servility of the house elves, which Hermione does her best to bring to an end.

Dursley family

Harry's cruel foster parents are Vernon and Petunia Dursley. Their gluttonous son is called Dudley. (Rowling thinks of him as something of a dud.) He's an eating (and a bullying) machine rather than a fully realised character. Their excessive attention to such a monstrosity (in all senses) gives added impact to their brutal treatment of Harry, who's almost under house arrest in **Privet Drive**.

Dursley is also the name of a town that Rowling felt carried the appropriate overtones of negativity, seeing the word as 'dull and forbidding'. The Dursleys glorify dull consumerism and a 'keeping up with the Joneses' mindset. They also personify philistinism in its most boorish form. This is even more reprehensible because of their knowledge that Harry has secret gifts. They indulge in wish fulfilment regarding his wizardry, apparently believing that if they ignore it for long enough he'll turn into a **Muggle** like them. Not! The fact that they live in dread of wizardry increases the dramatic impact of Harry's invitation to Hogwarts when he finally gets to see it.

Dursley, Marjorie

Aunt Marge is Vernon's portly sister. She's generally thought to be modelled on Rowling's grandmother, with whom Jo didn't get on as a child. In the books, Harry dreads her visits. Like Dudley, if not all the **Dursley family**, she's more a caricature than a real person. She abuses Harry so much on one occasion that he inflates her like a balloon and she flies around the room, screaming to be let down. Afterwards he berates himself for using magic on **Muggles** outside Hogwarts. He even fears expulsion (à la **Hagrid**). Thankfully, that doesn't transpire.

DVDs

The Chamber of Secrets was the fastest-selling DVD in UK history. Over a million copies of it flew over the counters of the world in just two days.

E

Edinburgh

Rowling's main home, though she has other properties in London and Perthshire. **Jessica** goes to school here, and Rowling herself occasionally even does some local shopping, though she has to be careful the paparazzi don't get wind of it beforehand.

Education

Before 'Harry Potter', **Emma Watson** (Hermione in the movies) admits that all she knew about magic was 'white rabbits and black hats'.

Elder Wand

The one Voldemort takes from Dumbledore's grave to kill Harry. Its allegiance to Harry, however, causes Voldemort's **Avada Kedavra** curse to backfire on himself after Harry casts an **Expelliarmus** spell.

Enervate

To bring somebody back to consciousness.

Engorgio

Spell used by **Alastor Moody** to enlarge a spider. The corollary is 'Reducio'.

Environment

Rowling says her ideal writing environment is 'a large café with a small corner table overlooking an interesting street that would serve strong coffee'. (That's the café, not the street!)

Erised

The Mirror of Erised first appears in *The Philosopher's Stone*. In it one can see one's most heartfelt desires reflected, a mirror image if you like, and Harry sees his parents. Written backwards, of course, 'Erised' spells 'desire'. (One is reminded of Dylan Thomas' fictional location 'Llareggub'). A message at the top of the mirror states 'Erised stra ehru oyt ube cafru oyt on wohsi'. If we say this backwards we get the sentence 'I show not your face but your heart's desire'.

What makes this episode so painful for Harry is the intangibility of the images he sees before him – so near and yet so far. He's never seen his parents before, and now here they are. Or are they? Seeing them but being unable to connect properly with them compounds his agony as it gives rise to an unfulfillable need.

Rowling said this chapter was the most heartbreaking she ever wrote as it reminded her of her own mother, who died young. Asked once in an interview what she herself might have seen in such a magic mirror, she joked, 'I can think of a particular journalist I'd like to see boiled in oil'. (A rather Ron Weasleyish comment, one would have thought.)

Evans, Lily

Harry's mother. Evans is her maiden name.

Evens, Bryony

Employee of Rowling's agent **Christopher Little** who first recognised her writing potential, though not even she could have envisaged the manner in which sales would snowball over the years.

Everybody Hurts

This was the song that got Rowling through her worst times when she was penniless and alone, with only an unpublished Harry for company.

Expanding boot

Arthur Weasley has one of these on his **Ford Anglia**. Every motorist's dream!

Expelliarmus

A spell that causes the victim's weapon to fly out of their hand. **Snape** uses it against **Gilderoy Lockhart** in *The Chamber of Secrets*.

Fame

Rowling knows she's been incredibly lucky in life. If someone had told her 10 years ago that she would be an esteemed guest at Downing Street, Buckingham Palace and the White House, she would have laughed them out of the room. As Lana Whited wrote in the book *The Ivory Tower and Harry Potter*, 'It is difficult to recall another occasion when the public was so enraptured by an author's work since Americans stood on the wharves of Boston Harbour awaiting the latest instalment of **Charles Dickens**' *The Old Curiosity Shop*. But there's a downside too. As Rowling puts it: 'I never expected to be photographed on a beach through long lenses. I didn't think they'd rake through my bins.' She now knows there are a lot of **Rita Skeeters** out there.

Rupert Grint says, 'I still have to clean my own room.' And here's **Emma Watson**'s take on it: 'Some people stare at you as if you're some kind of zoo animal.'

Family trees

Rowling is exhaustive about these. When David Heyman was producing *The Order of the Phoenix* he asked her if she could give him some information on **Sirius Black**'s lineage. 'Within fifteen minutes,' he says, 'she sent us a fax going back through six generations of the Blacks with about 100 names, birthdays, death dates, who married whom, and even how names were pronounced.'

Fan clubs

Some years ago a woman from Glasgow enquired how she might go about joining the Harry Potter Fan Club. She was 60 years of age.

Fang

This is the aggressive name of **Hagrid**'s boarhound, which is actually quite tame unless provoked. His three-headed dog **Fluffy**, in contrast, sounds tame but is actually savage. Maybe Rowling doesn't want us to get too smug as regards her 'sound equals sense' patterns of naming things.

Fans
Rowling says some of her fans are so 'into' her books they perhaps know more about their convolutions than she does. She gets upwards of a thousand fan letters a week.

Fat Friar
The house ghost of **Hufflepuff**. He forms friendships with the Hogwarts students, unlike most other ghosts, but is driven barmy by **Peeves** and holds meetings with the express purpose of trying to get rid of him.

Fat Lady
The portrait of the Fat Lady guards the dormitories in **Gryffindor**. When she refuses to let **Sirius Black** in, he slashes it to smithereens.

Fathers
Most of the Harry Potter books, Rowling feels, read like a litany of bad fathers. Perhaps this is due to the fact that she had problems with **Jessica**'s father, and also her own, particularly when he remarried so soon after Rowling's mother died.

Fawkes

This is Dumbledore's pet phoenix. He's probably named after Guy Fawkes, with whom we associate fireworks. The phoenix, of course, rises from ashes, another fiery connection.

Feather-Light

A spell Harry thinks of using to make his trunk light enough to carry on his broomstick when he's running away from the **Dursley family** in *The Prisoner of Azkaban*.

Felix Felicis

A potion that Harry brews to win an award in *The Half-Blood Prince* (Hermione calls it 'liquid luck'.) It's also given to Harry by **Horace Slughorn** in that book.

Felton, Tom

Felton is the actor who plays **Draco Malfoy** in the movies, and he appears to be a bigger hit with the ladies than **Daniel Radcliffe**, which disappoints Rowling. Why are women always attracted to the wrong kind of man? (Perhaps she was too – in her Portuguese husband.) This isn't so much a case of 'Treat 'em mean, keep 'em keen' as the attractive edge of danger exuded by any villain, all the way from Lucifer to Darth Vader. As the man said, virtue isn't always photogenic. And aesthetics overrides ethics when the whiff of cordite is present.

Feminism

Many readers feel Rowling should have struck a blow for feminism by writing about 'Harriet Potter' instead of Harry. She can appreciate the point but felt she could put herself better into the role of Hermione – who's brighter academically than Harry. She does give him the thick **glasses** she herself wore as a child, however, and the same birthday: 31 July. On a more general level, she has girls as well as boys excelling at **Quidditch**, and Hermione pleading for equal rights for elves, and even refusing to eat a certain meal at one point when she hears it's been prepared by them. She refuses to accept Ron's point that elves like being ordered about the place. (**Winky** is alone in this.) She despises slavery in any shape or form and starts the Society for the Promotion of Elfish Welfare (SPEW) to try and put them on an equal footing.

In another sense, we can see elements of many female fictional and fairytale characters in Harry, all the way from Cinderella through the Sleeping Beauty, Little Red Riding Hood, Jane Eyre and even Rapunzel, who has to escape from quite a different place than a **cupboard**.

In an essay called 'Blue Wizards and Pink Witches', author Elizabeth Heilman suggests that making the girls good at

Quidditch is mere tokenism on Rowling's part because they're not **Seekers** and therefore don't impact significantly on the results of games. **Cho Chang** is a Seeker but even she plays second fiddle to Harry in this role.

Heilman goes on to say that Hermione has to have a 'makeover' in *The Goblet of Fire* to qualify as **Viktor Krum**'s date for the ball. As a tomboy who wasn't interested in prettifying herself, Heilman suggests, she wouldn't have made the Cinderella transformation that intrigued Krum. The Veelas, she says, are even worse, being little more than 'male fantasy sex objects able to seduce, beguile and confuse males.' **Emma Watson**, who plays Hermione in the movies, herself admitted that the ball scene in *The Goblet of Fire* was the hardest one she had to do 'because usually they're trying to make me look as geeky as possible' and here they dispensed with the 'frizzy-haired, woolly-sweater-wearing nerd' she usually is.

Feminists even blame Rowling for using initials instead of her Christian name on her books, thereby rendering them androgynous and, in their minds, returning literature to an era when women had to write under pseudonyms to get published. This was a decision that was mooted by her publisher, who probably rightly deduced that she'd be cutting off a lot of her potential readership by invading a hitherto all-male genre. As Edmund Kern wrote in *The Wisdom of Harry Potter*, the adventures of Harriet Potter would not have been as popular as those of Harry even if they included her sidekicks faithful 'Rona' Weasley or brainy 'Hermes' Granger.

As far as feminists are concerned, all of this speculation about success is beside the point. But Rowling feels that her saleability enables her to exert clout in the world in different ways. If she'd been an unsuccessful novelist going by the name of Jo Rowling she wouldn't have been able to give such significant amounts of money to Comic Relief, single parents associations or the Multiple Sclerosis Society. Idealism is all very well, but sometimes you have to go in the publisher's door to come out of your own.

Fernunculus

Spell that causes a rash of boils to appear on a victim's face.

Fidelius Charm

This is deployed to hide a secret from everyone but a Secret-Keeper. Harry's parents used it to protect themselves from Voldemort, but **Peter Pettigrew** was the Keeper in that instance and of course betrayed them.

Figg, Arabella

This is the local woman from **Little Whinging** – her house smells of cats and overcooked cabbage – who used to take care of Harry when the **Dursley family** were out. But this is no ordinary neighbour; she's actually a member of the **Order of the Phoenix** chosen especially by Dumbledore to see that Harry is okay.

Filch, Argus

The argus is a creature from Greek mythology with a thousand eyes. Rowling probably chose this name because the Hogwarts caretaker is a meddlesome busybody who makes it his business to see everything that's going on. 'Filch' is also appropriate because he's forever confiscating things.

Finite Incantata

A Charm that **Snape** uses to keep his students quiet.

Firenze

This centaur, who used to live in the **Forbidden Forest**, can read the future from the movements of the planets. He once saved Harry's life, and later taught **Divination** at Hogwarts. (Dumbledore made the classroom look like a forest to make him feel at home.) His name is the Italian for Florence. The famous astronomer Galileo is buried there, which perhaps accounts for Rowling giving him this name.

Flame-Freezing Charm

Self-explanatory spell used by medieval wizards that crops up in *The Prisoner of Azkaban*.

Flamel, Nicolas

This character, an alchemist in *The Philosopher's Stone*, is over 600 years old, as is his wife. He suddenly becomes mortal when the stone is lost. (He still didn't do too badly age-wise!) Dumbledore tells Harry at one point that he will die before he reaches the age of 666. Significantly, this is the number of the Biblical Anti-Christ.

Nicholas Flamel was a real person reputed to have had the Midas Touch, creating the stone in his laboratory in 1382. (This means that Rowling is about right with his age considering her books are set in the present.) His wife was called Perenelle, as she is in the books. It's said that he only used the gold he created three times, and that he did so not for his own benefit (he lived frugally) but for others'. With his money he built hospitals and churches, and also gave help to the needy. When he died, looters allegedly broke into his home looking for gold. Finding none, they opened his coffin and found it empty. So maybe his stone not only held the secret of converting metal to gold, but of immortality as well!

Flat life

At 27 and reeling from a broken marriage, Rowling had to scrimp to get a deposit for somewhere to live. Of the place in which she ended up she said, 'The best thing you could say about it was that it had a roof. If I concentrated hard enough I was able to block out the sounds of mice behind the skirting board.'

Flint, Marcus

Captain of the **Slytherin Quidditch** team.

Flitwick, Filius

The Charms professor at Hogwarts and the head of **Ravenclaw**. Like many characters in Rowling's books he's named after an English town. Rowling generally describes him in very effeminate terms. As Elizabeth Heilman wrote in her essay 'Blue Wizards and Pink Witches', 'He's characterised with words and images that are connotative of crude cultural stereotypes of gay men.' Hmm.

Floo powder

If you throw this into a fireplace connected to the Floo network and then step into the flames, you can travel anywhere you like afterwards.

Flourish & Blotts

This is the bookshop to end all bookshops in **Diagon Alley**. Its publication *The Monster Book of Monsters* has a cover that bites anyone who picks it up. Its book *The Invisible Book of Invisibility* is, you've guessed it, invisible. (You have to give it to Flourish & Blotts for consistency.)

Fluffy

Hagrid's dog, who's based on Cerberus, the three-headed dog that guarded Hades in Greek mythology. Orpheus rescued his love Eurydice by playing music to tame Cerberus, and this is what Hermione does to send Fluffy to sleep in *The Philosopher's Stone*. Hagrid bought him from 'a Greek chappie' – another nod to Greek mythology.

Football

Rowling says she once dated a fanatical Chelsea fan, their relationship totally revolving around the fortunes of that particular football club. 'They got relegated and we split up,' she reveals, 'then they had a fantastic season and we got together again.' (No wonder she invented **Quidditch** as an antidote).

Forbidden Forest

This comes into *The Philosopher's Stone*, but forests crop up in many works of fantasy. There's the dark forest of

The Wizard of Oz and **Tolkien**'s Fangorn Forest, and of course Hansel and Gretel get lost in a forest as well.

Ford Anglia

The car **Percy Weasley** drives to help Harry escape from the **Dursley family** in *The Chamber of Secrets*. It's Mr Weasley's flying car and owes something to Ian Fleming's Chitty Chitty Bang Bang in concept. In real life Rowling also travelled in a turquoise Ford Anglia with her childhood friend Seán Harris, upon whom Ron is based. (She dedicated that book to him, calling him her 'getaway driver and foulweather friend'.) This was her broomstick on wheels, if you like – the means by which she escaped from routine in a desolate area where little happened. Her books are chock-a-block with such details, providing biographers with telling clues like the breadcrumbs Hansel and Gretel dropped on the way to the ginger-bread house in the famous fairytale.

Foresight

Rowling, unlike Professor **Trelawney**, doesn't have a crystal ball, but she knew from the start of her Harry Potter career that there would be seven novels. If she writes an eighth book, she says, it will be a kind of reference book for the other seven and all royalties will go to charity.

Forest, Antonia

Ron's family background, as has often been pointed out, is quite similar to that of the twins in Forest's *Autumn Term*.

France

The English language edition of *The Order of the Phoenix* became the only English language book to ever top the best-seller list in this country.

Freedom

This is a theme running through all of the books. Harry frees **Dobby**, the house elf, as well as the boa constrictor in the zoo. He also frees himself by confronting the ghosts of his past head on, and by escaping from the 11-year stranglehold of the **Dursleys**.

Frenemies

This American jargon term expresses the manner in which Hermione falls in and out of friendship with Harry and Ron before the trio become well-nigh inseparable.

Fry, Stephen

The narrator of the Harry Potter audio tapes. He did a reading of *The Philosopher's Stone* on the radio on Boxing

Day in 1997 that went on for a staggering eight hours. It pulled in over 3.5 million listeners.

Fudge, Cornelius

The bumbling, fumbling, Minister of Magic. He's well named because he's always trying to 'fudge' issues rather than confronting them head on.

Future, The

Predicting the future is a very difficult business indeed, as Dumbledore likes to remind us, but Ms Rowling is determined that there will be no-post Hogwarts Harry suffering from midlife crisis, or whatever.

Fwooper

This is a bird whose singing causes insanity.

Gabrielle

Fleur Delacour's sister.

Gadgetry

We would all like to have dishes that wash themselves, as **Molly Weasley** does, or the ability to blow up an obnoxious aunt (or even a more obnoxious cousin). We'd all like to own a **Put-Outer** or **Time-Turner** or Daydream Potion or any of the other innumerable items Rowling puts before us in her books. By presenting them to us in a lackadaisical fashion she taps into every child's wish to live in a fantasy world. She's not the first author to do this and she won't be the last, but the sheer range and diversity of her gadgets is where a lot of her literary inventiveness lies.

Galleons

These, along with Sickles and Knuts, are the currency in which Harry's money is kept in **Gringotts**. A galleon is worth 17 Sickles and a Sickle is worth 29 Knuts.

Gallico, Paul

Gallico is the author of *Manxmouse* (1986) and another acknowledged influence on Rowling.

Gambol & Japes

The **wizard** joke shop, offering all forms of exotic novelties. Once again, the playful words conjure up the items on display.

Gambon, Michael

The man who replaced **Richard Harris** as Dumbledore in the movies after Harris died. Ian McKellen was the producers' first choice, but he was suffering from 'Lord of the Rings withdrawal' so passed it up.

Gardner's Crescent, 28

This is the address of the one-bedroom flat in Edinburgh where Rowling lived on a shoestring with her daughter as she put the finishing touches to her first book. It might in time become a shrine.

Gaunt, Merope

The witch who became Tom Riddle's wife after he fell under the spell of a love potion she prepared for him, but he deserted her after its effects wore off. By this time she was pregnant with his son **Tom Marvolo Riddle** (i.e. **Voldemort**). She gave birth to him in an orphanage but died soon afterwards, having lost the will to live.

Genres

Rowling doesn't really see herself as a writer of fantasies. In the classic fantasy the world of magic is a yellow brick road leading to a pot of gold at the end of the rainbow, but magic for Harry creates as many problems as it solves. 'I like subverting genres,' she once claimed. Fellow author Terry Pratchett subsequently had a go at her, saying sarcastically, 'I would have thought the wizards, witches, trolls, unicorns and hidden worlds would have given her an idea of the genre she was operating in.'

Maybe this is to miss the point. Rowling has mixed different genre elements into her books. They're part fable, part public school whimsy, part **bildungsroman**, even part detective story. They're not whodunits in the Sherlock

Holmes/Hercule Poirot sense because we know who the villain is from Book One, but they're 'why-did-he-do-its', which is much more interesting. There's also that intriguing 'doppleganger' thing going between Harry and Voldemort. Both of them are **Parselmouths**, both use similar **wands** and there's even a physical resemblance between Harry and **Tom Riddle**. A part of Voldemort entered Harry when he tried to kill him as a child, as we learn from *The Deathly Hallows*.

Gerber, Michael

Gerber has made himself a small fortune churning out parodies of the Harry Potter books. They cause some Rowling-lovers mirth and others outrage. Harry becomes Barry Trotter, Hogwarts is Hogwash, Dumbledore is Bumblemore, The Dursleys are the Dimslys, Hagrid is Hafwid, Voldemort is Valumart, and so on. Gerber's books have self-deprecating titles like *Barry Trotter and the Shameless Parody* and *Barry Trotter and the Unnecessary Sequel*. The latter bears the subtitle, 'The book nobody has been waiting for!' On the inside cover, after stating that it has no endorsement by Rowling, **Warner Brothers** or **Bloomsbury**, Gerber adds impishly, 'Of course this notice itself could be parodic, in which case it's anybody's guess as to what the hell is going on.'

The book, he adds, has been published by Victor Gollancz, which he describes as a 'cynical, money-grubbing imprint of the Orion Publishing Group' and has been 'grudgingly' printed by Clays Ltd. On the dust jacket his hobbies are listed as 'solitaire, hypochondria and sleeping'. Rowling can console herself that imitation is the sincerest form of flattery.

Gifts

When **Emma Watson** was asked what her ideal wizard gift would be, she replied: 'An **owl**, because it's cheaper than texting.'

Gillyweed

Dobby gives this to Harry to enable him to breathe under water during the **Triwizard Tournament** in *The Goblet of Fire*.

Glasses

Heroes don't usually wear glasses so Rowling is trying to break down a stereotype here. (**Michael Caine**, her aforementioned favourite actor, did the same for adults in the Harry Palmer spy series.) She has her hero bespectacled because she was fed up with the brainy one in novels, rather than the brave one, always wearing glasses.

So Harry, not the most academic student at Hogwarts, gets them. Of course they also dramatise the change that occurs when the mild-mannered **wizard** realises he has super powers.

Goblet of Fire

This is the title of the third book and also a healing vessel something like the Holy Grail of Arthurian legend. Rowling was originally going to call it 'The **Triwizard Tournament**' but changed it because she felt the new title had more of a 'ring of destiny' to it – which is, of course, the central theme.

Goblins

These work at **Gringotts**.

Godric's Hollow

Fictional village named after **Godric Gryffindor**.

Goudge, Elizabeth

Goudge's *The Little White Horse* was Rowling's favourite book as a child. Like her own work it has animals that can change their shapes, and an orphan (female) who enters a magical world through a rocky structure, emerging into a castle where she finds she has a secret identity.

Goyle, Gregory

One of **Draco Malfoy**'s rather dim bodyguards at Hogwarts.

GrandPré, Mary

Illustrator of the US editions of the Harry Potter books.

Granger, Hermione

Harry's friend and ally (though they have their flare-ups betimes) is a chatty young girl so it's appropriate that she's named after the Greek Goddess of Harmony and Concord. She's turned to stone in *Chamber of Secrets* just like her namesake in Shakespeare's *A Winter's Tale*. When we first meet her she strikes us as the kind of person we would have hated at school – the one who always put her hand up first and had her homework done almost before it was set. As the series goes on, however, she becomes more likeable as she sets herself more human priorities and loses her know-all persona. (Her friendship with Harry and Ron takes off after they rescue her from the troll in Book One). Rowling modelled Hermione on herself in many ways, though Rowling wasn't as arrogant. We can see Hermione's egalitarian principles in the manner in which she campaigns for the freedom of the house elves. We learn precious little about her dentist parents apart from the fact that they brought her to France on holiday one year. She seems to get on better with boys than girls. Hermione finally marries Ron, as we learn in the epilogue to **The Deathly Hallows**.

Grawp

Hagrid's half-brother, who's even taller than him. Hagrid protects him when **Dolores Umbridge** harasses him.

Great Hall

This is the central meeting point at Hogwarts.

Gregorovitch

European **wand**-maker.

Greyback, Fenrir

Character who turns himself into a wolf in **The Half-Blood Prince**. (Fenrir is an old wolf from Norse mythology.)

Grey Lady

The house ghost at **Ravenclaw**.

Grimmauld Place

The house of **Sirius Black** and the **Order of the Phoenix**. There's also a Harry Potter website named after it.

Grims

These huge dogs, which are portents of death, terrorise Harry in *The Prisoner of Azkaban*.

Gringotts

This is the **Wizard** Bank where Harry's parents have deposited money for him. It comes from the word 'ingot', which is a bar of gold.

Grint, Rupert

Grint appeared in school plays as characters like Peter Pan and Rumplestiltskin before landing the role of Ron in the movies. He hadn't done any professional acting, which makes his naturalness in front of the camera all the more remarkable. He did his audition in the form of a rap number, which seems to have swung it for him – thespian wannabes take note.

Grubbly-Plank, Wilhelmina

This lady is the substitute professor for Care of Magical Creatures, filling in for **Hagrid** when he's absent.

Gryffindor

Harry's Hogwarts residence, with the core values of loyalty and bravery, literally means 'golden griffin'. A griffin is a fabled creature that's part lion and part eagle, which explains why its animal symbol is a lion.

Gryffindor, Godric

One of the four founders of Hogwarts.

Gryndilows

These are legendary water demons.

Guilt

Rowling felt guilty for devoting so much of her time to writing when her daughter **Jessica** was a baby and times were hard. 'You can't eat paper,' she remarked.

Hagrid, Rubeus

This gentle giant, one of the most likeable characters in the series, was expelled from Hogwarts as a young man for being found guilty of misusing his magic powers. (The reality of the situation was that he was framed by **Tom Riddle** for opening the Chamber of Secrets). He subsequently became Keeper of the Keys and Grounds and Gamekeeper before finally landing a post as lecturer on the Care of Magical Creatures in Hogwarts. (This career is almost over before it starts when **Draco Malfoy** ruins his first class.)

Hagrid's mother deserted him when he was three and his father died when he was a teenager. 'Rubeus' means ruddy and Hagrid is a term used in Newfoundland to describe someone who has become 'hag-ridden'. It conveys his raggedy appearance and general off-beat personality. He's a rough diamond who's his own worst enemy, becoming frustrated by his mistakes. Sometimes he doesn't know his own strength, but he wouldn't willingly hurt a fly.

Thomas Hardy uses the term 'hagrid' in *The Mayor of Casterbridge* so it was also in Britain at that time (probably meaning 'harassed'). Hagrid does get harassed, though he's entitled to because of the scars of his past. He's generally good-humoured, however, and speaks in a folksy dialect, a mixture of cockney and the West Country. He likes his alcohol a little too much and isn't hugely intelligent – as he proves when he allows himself to be duped by the 'Greek chap' into giving away the secret of how to get past **Fluffy** – but he has a heart of gold and supports our three main characters to the wire. One of his most eccentric traits is his inability to see how huge creatures can be fearsome and dangerous. Considering he's so huge himself, maybe they seem puny to him. As a boy he even raised werewolf cubs. Hagrid is also the name of a medieval saint, and Rowling says he's the character she would most like to meet in real life.

Half-Blood Prince, The

Harry Potter and the Half-Blood Prince, Rowling's penultimate Harry Potter novel, flew off the shelves faster than a hot-wired broomstick, as one commentator observed, selling over seven million copies on the first day of its publication in the US. At its launch in New York, the Barnes & Noble bookshop was transformed into Hogwarts for the evening, with **wand**-wielding witches, owls, Harry lookalikes with round specs and various other exotic creatures parading around with their new title under their oxters. Some critics dismissed the book as being too slow-moving, too samey and with not enough bite, but all agreed that it picked up momentum as it went along, and the death of Dumbledore set things up nicely for a final confrontation between Harry and Voldemort. It was also refreshing to see the relationship between Harry and **Ginny Weasley** developing, and the background story on Voldemort was long overdue.

Harris, Ellie

The grand-daughter of **Richard Harris**, who persuaded him to take the role of Dumbledore after he'd turned it down. She told him she'd never speak to him again if he didn't change his mind. He gave in to her eventually, having mellowed from the wild man he used to be in his youth. His energy level was low, but he only had to work 20 days in the six months of the shoot, which helped. Harris grew to love the role and even secured a little part for Ellie herself in the Hogwarts banquet scene.

Harris, Richard

Harris played Dumbledore in the first two Harry Potter movies. He was very ill with Hodgkin's disease (cancer of the lymph glands) during the second one but refused to see a doctor until shooting had finished. After his initial reluctance to take the role, Harris ended up giving it Lear-like reverberations and endearing himself to a whole generation of filmgoers who wouldn't previously have known of his stellar achievements. The last scene he played in *The Chamber of Secrets* was especially poignant because of his illness. The crew sussed it was probably going to be his celluloid swansong.

This is how Harris' biographer Michael Feeney Callan summed it up: 'He addresses the gathered clan and passes the decree permitting a holiday from homework. The camera pulls back from the febrile, cheering faces, swoops over his regal shoulder and zooms up from the fairytale castle into a blemishless starry sky. He has given us reason to laugh, then exited in a sprinkle of fairy dust.' Harris told **Christopher Columbus**, the director, that he'd kill him if he didn't keep him on for the next Potter venture (he was given to such jocular threats) but sadly died long before *The Prisoner of Azkaban* was made.

Hedwig

This is the owl that **Hagrid** gives Harry as a gift. She's finally felled by a stray Killing Curse in ***The Deathly Hallows***.

Hippogriff

A creature from *The Prisoner of Azkaban* that's a hybrid of bird, griffin and horse.

Hoffman, Dustin

Rowling developed a crush on this diminutive star after seeing the film *Little Big Man* – an appropriate title under the circumstances.

Hogsmeade

Wizard village visited by Hogwarts students. Harry is prohibited because **Sirius Black** is on the loose but still finds his way to it, thanks to the **Marauder's Map**.

Hogwarts

This school of wizardry is an anagram of 'ghost war', though nobody is sure if this is mere coincidence or more game-playing on Rowling's part. It's situated in a castle on a hill beside a lake and a forest: a classic location for a fantasy tale. (When Rowling was nine, her parents moved to a village near Chepstow in South Wales, which also had a castle on a hill.)

Hogwarts is a thousand years old and isn't visible on any map. It was built as a hideaway for **wizards** from **Muggles**, who were giving them some grief at the time. Four wizards were behind it: **Godric Gryffindor**, Helga Hufflepuff, **Rowena Ravenclaw** and **Salazar Slytherin** – hence the names of the four houses. Rowling probably took 'Salazar' from the Portuguese dictator of the same name. She doesn't have a map of Hogwarts – nobody could, because furniture, books, rooms, staircases, etc. are continually moving – but she says she knows where everything is at a given time. (Would a **Marauder's Map** not help, Joanne?)

Honeydukes
The sweet shop in **Hogsmeade**.

Hooch, Rolanda
The lady in charge of **Quidditch** and flying lessons. Or should I say lesson. As somebody pointed out, she only seems to give one!

Horcrux

A horcrux is a receptacle into which a person discards part of their soul so that they will be preserved in some form when they die. It's a banned subject at Hogwarts but **Horace Slughorn** told the young Voldemort about it after repeated questioning from him and he's had a guilt complex about this ever since.

Voldemort split his soul into seven pieces and put six of them into horcruxes. A horcrux, by the way, can only be made when one is in the act of killing. (They are not, repeat not, created by nice people.) Harry himself is the seventh horcrux as part of Voldemort's spirit escaped into him when he killed Harry's parents. This is why Harry alone can kill him, using the **Elder Wand** to reverse Voldemort's own spell on him.

Horowitz, Anthony

Some commentators have listed Horowitz's *Groosham Grange*, also set in a **boarding school**, as a strong influence on Rowling's work.

Hover Charm

A charm used to make an object float in the air. It's similar to the Levitation Charm.

Howler

Wizard mail that self-destructs after giving its message. The espionage tapes in the 'Mission Impossible' series used to do this too, but Howlers actually burst into flames.

Hufflepuff

The Hogwarts house that emphasises industry and hard work. It was founded by Helga Hufflepuff and its animal emblem is the badger. 'Hufflepuff' is an onomatopoeic term.

Identification

Rowling said as she was writing *The Deathly Hallows*: 'For years now people have asked me whether I ever dream that I'm in Harry's world. The answer was "No" until a few nights ago, when I had an epic dream in which I was simultaneously Harry and the narrator.' In the dream the staff in the café where she wrote the book were roaming round on giant stilts. 'Maybe I should cut back on the caffeine,' Rowling concluded.

Image

Rowling hates being photographed with broomsticks. She says it makes her feel like a twat.

Impedimenta

Spell used to immobilise somebody. Ron uses one in *The Goblet of Fire* to stop a bee in mid-air. The other such spells are Petrificus Totalus and Stupefy. Harry uses Impedimenta on the giant spider in the same book, and Madam Hooch uses it in *The Order of the Phoenix* to break up a fight between Harry and **Draco Malfoy**.

Imperius Curse

A curse that enables a **wizard** to control the mind and body of another, as happens with Voldemort and **Quirrell**. It's one of the **Unforgivable Curses**.

Impervius

Hermione puts this spell on Harry's **glasses** to make them resist water when his form dips due to lack of visibility during a rainy game of **Quidditch**.

Inconsistencies

Harry Potter devotee Alexander Wang has pointed out a number of these in the books. Why, he asks, don't the Weasleys perform magic to make themselves more financially secure? Also, why aren't there 'regular' classes at Hogwarts in subjects like English and Maths? Third, considering Harry has had such a dysfunctional upbringing, how is he so normal and idealistic? Wang also wonders why

Harry's parents aren't ghosts at Hogwarts like, say, **Nearly Headless Nick**. These are all very legitimate puzzlers, but it's also true that the books would probably be less interesting if such situations applied. (It's called poetic licence.)

In her essay 'Crowning the King', author Farah Mendlessohn wonders why the Weasleys are poor in the first place considering that Arthur has a pretty good civil service job and two older children doing quite well for themselves. She also points out a more subtle inconsistency to do with **Quidditch**: 'When the Malfoys present the **Slytherin** team with new brooms, this is regarded as cheating, yet when Harry receives a high-powered broom it is framed as simply good fortune that rectifies a perceived injustice. No comment is made that he now outpowers the competing **Seekers**.' It would be interesting to hear how Rowling (who's hard to catch out on plotty intricacies) would respond to these allegations.

Inspiration

Rowling became a writer, she once said, because she was bored with her own life and wanted to escape into those of others. Many other authors would share this feeling.

Internet

Rowling finds this fascinating: 'Typing your thoughts into the ether and getting answers back from strangers.' It can also, needless to say, be extremely dangerous – especially for children. (Or world-famous authors susceptible to dangerous stalkers.)

The internet was instrumental in the international success of Rowling's books from the point of view of transmitting UK excitement so speedily. Because of early fan sites, chat rooms, gossip, etc., the original readers conveyed their fascination to their American counterparts and this made **Scholastic**, the American publishers, sit up and take notice. The large sum they paid for the US rights was way out of proportion to what a publisher would normally pay for an unknown children's author, so perhaps Rowling has the internet 'traffic' to thank for her good fortune in this regard.

One of the ironic things about her career is that, when it began, she was commended for getting children away from computers and back to the 'archaic' delight of turning pages, but now that she's become such a resounding success, a lot of the discussions about her works take place on the very computers she originally supplanted.

A related irony is that Rowling started off by gate-crashing a male genre, but in subsequent years it became almost mandatory to be seen with a Harry Potter novel under one's arm. It became a badge of honour, as it were, and peer pressure was exerted on many children to 'join the pack' rather than be seen reading anything else. It all became like literary snobbery for neophytes, and that's still going on today as children boast about how many Harry Potter novels they've read. To this extent she took children away from other genres.

Many people would argue that she's over-read today, to the exclusion of better, lesser-known scribes. But this was always the way in literature. There's always a John Grisham or a Stephen King outstripping the opposition by a country mile. Nothing succeeds like success.

Interviews
Emma Watson doesn't have much respect for these. 'Everyone asks the same questions,' she claims, 'and you just stand there like a broken record going "La la la la la".'

Invisibility Cloak
This is self-explanatory. Harry wears it in *The Philosopher's Stone* when he doesn't want to be spotted by **Filch**. He also uses it to eavesdrop on conversations. It was left to

him by his father. In Greek mythology, Hades, the God of the underworld, had a Cap of Darkness that served the same purpose. (Hades means 'the unseen one' in ancient Greek.) Only 'Mad Eye' **Moody** can see through it in the Harry Potter series.

Irony

Rowling uses a lot of this in her work, particularly when writing about the **Dursley family**. Their self-satisfied airs contrast markedly with her own ill-disguised contempt for them, couched in restrained language.

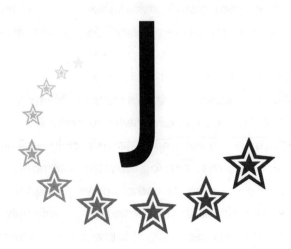

Jessica

This is the name of Rowling's daughter, who was a very small child during most of the compositions of the early books. She named her after Jessica Mitford, one of her favourite childhood authors. (Mitford ran away from home at the age of 19 to join the Spanish Civil War and has as a result always been something of a role model for Rowling. She was also a pretty good writer.) If Jessica had been born male, Rowling says, she would have called her Harry, though she would then have had to change the name of her hero, as she wouldn't have wanted her son to carry that kind of baggage through life.

The first two words Jessica uttered, according to her mother, were – perhaps not too surprisingly – 'Harry' and 'Potter'.

Jesus Christ

Many Fundamentalist Christians have problems with the Harry Potter books, regarding them as potentially dangerous hocus-pocus affairs for impressionable children. This is a rather alarmist over-reaction for most common-sensical readers, who see them as enthralling yarns exploring the tussle between good and evil while having some jolly good fun along the way. Ironically, there are many similarities between Harry and Jesus, who was also spared from death as a baby, was raised by foster parents and went about his father's business just before he became a teenager. He was betrayed, had secret powers and confronted a demonic nemesis. The Holy Grail from which Jesus drank at the Last Supper also has echoes in Rowling's **Goblet of Fire**, and Harry ('The Boy Who Lived') is referred to as 'The Chosen One'. Could we even go so far as to say the lightning scar on his forehead is reminiscent of the mark of Cain?

Johnson, Angelina
A **Gryffindor Chaser**.

Jordan, Lee

Lee is a commentator on **Gryffindor** matches and also a friend of the Weasley twins.

Jorkins, Bertha

A Hogwarts student who was killed by Voldemort in 1994.

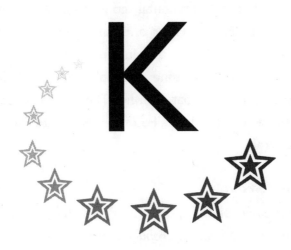

K

Karkaroff, Igor
The headmaster of **Durmstrang** school, this **Death Eater** turns in his colleagues to **Azkaban** prison to save his own skin.

King, Stephen
Rowling has often been referred to as 'Stephen King for kids'. He's an avowed admirer of her works and has gone out to bat for her any time she's been accused of being derivative or complacent.

King's Cross
This station figures prominently in all the

books. It has a sentimental connection for Rowling because her parents, Peter and Anne, met on a **train** here. He was on his way to join the Royal Navy and she to become a WREN. Anne was cold so Peter gallantly offered to share his coat with her. The romance took off from there. A year later, Peter proposed to Anne on another train.

Kloves, Steve

The screenwriter for the Harry Potter movies. Rowling admired his work in *The Fabulous Baker Boys*, one of her favourite films, but was apprehensive about him 'ripping my babies apart' when he got cracking on her own work. A wise young reader once said that she preferred books to films 'because the scenery is nicer'. She was alluding to the fact that the imagination can conjure up images that no camera can. Now that we've seen **Daniel Radcliffe**, **Rupert Grint**, **Emma Watson** and other actors, our perceptions of Rowling's characters are indelibly fixed in our minds, and that has to be some kind of a sacrifice. It was also part of the reason Rowling was wary of meeting Kloves.

The pair of them, however, hit it off immediately and now get on famously. They seem to have an intuitive under-standing of what has to be kept in and what has to go out, film being a primarily visual medium. A writer, they say, would sooner kill their mother than part with a semi-colon, but Rowling understands the need for shrinkage in the transition from page to stage. 'If my books weren't pruned for the screen,' she says with that dry wit for which she's famous, 'the films would all be 24 hours long.' Which might be a problem for viewers looking for the last bus home.

Knight Bus

This is the magic bus that rescues Harry in the first book when he's stranded and alone after leaving **Privet Drive** in a rage. Rowling named its driver and conductor (Ernie and Stanley) after her grandfathers. Stanley's surname is Shunpike, another one of those compound terms (**trains** 'shun' turnpikes) Rowling delights in. Ernie's surname is Prang, which is a colloquial term meaning 'to collide with a car'. This is apt in the circumstances as his driving is so precarious. Objects like trees have to leap out of his way as he approaches. Since the bus travels at night, the 'k' is silent.

Knockturn Alley

Like **Diagon Alley**, this is another pun: a synonym for 'nocturnal' to get across the dark and dangerous overtones of the place. It first crops up in *The Chamber of Secrets*.

Kreacher
Sirius Black's servant.

Krum, Viktor
The Bulgarian **Quidditch** player who takes Hermione to the Yule Ball.

Kwikspell
Crash course in magic desired by **Argus Filch**.

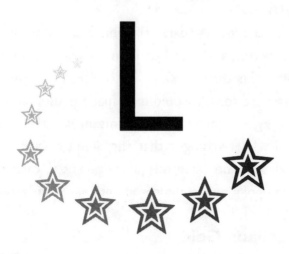

Langlock

The spell that glues a person's tongue to the roof of their mouth.

Le Guin, Ursula

Le Guin's *A Wizard of Earthsea* is often cited as an influence on Rowling.

Leaky Cauldron

The dingy pub that leads to **Diagon Alley**. When Harry goes into its courtyard and taps the brick that's three up and two across from the dustbin with his **wand**, it's open sesame time for him to reach his brave new world.

Length

Some people feel the early 'slimline' Harry Potter books were superior, and that less is more with Rowling. She herself admits that *The Order of the Phoenix*, for example, was a tad too long. 'I would have made it shorter if I had the energy,' she joked. What she meant was that she was so tired while writing it that she didn't have her usual editorial discipline. Fame was just beginning to catch up on her at this point, and to cut inroads into her writing routines.

Leprechaun Gold

The currency Ludo Bagman uses to pay **Fred and George Weasley** after they win their bet in the World Cup in 1994, but it soon disappears, being leprechaun gold.

Lestrange, Bellatrix

Death Eater who tortures **Neville Longbottom**'s parents and kills her cousin **Sirius Black**. She's the sister of **Narcissa Malfoy**. She's finally killed by **Molly Weasley** in *The Deathly Hallows*.

Lewis, C S

Another influence on Rowling. His Narnia Chronicles also have a central character called Digory (although there's only one 'g', unlike Rowling's **Cedric Diggory**).

Little, Christopher

Little is Rowling's agent. She was so delighted when he agreed to represent her that she read his letter of acceptance no less than eight times. The length of the book she sent him, *The Philosopher's Stone*, was 80 000 words. Since 40 000 words was the preferred maximum for children's books and she was an unpublished author it was a big leap of faith on his part. But his confidence was repaid a hundredfold.

Little sent the manuscript to 12 publishers without success (Transworld, HarperCollins, Penguin, etc. all passed), but after **Bloomsbury** took it on it wasn't too long before the US offered a six-figure sum for the rights. As for length, *The Philosopher's Stone* is now relatively anorexic in comparison to its successors. (*The Order of the Phoenix* weighs in at 125 000 words and children queued up in their droves to read it – which goes to show you how much publishers know about child psychology.)

Little Hangleton

The location of Riddle House.

Little Whinging

The village where the **Dursley family** live.

Lockhart, Gilderoy

The narcissistic teacher of Defence Against the **Dark Arts** (the most undesirable job in Hogwarts!) also fancies himself as an author and a magician, two activities he's singularly unsuited to. His main 'talent' is for flamboyance and self-projection, dressing like Liberace and even carrying autographed pictures of himself in his pocket. He always goes for the main chance and is all bluff and bluster, managing to win the 'Witch Weekly Most Charming Smile' Award five years running. Rowling's jibes at him are really attacks on the vacuousness of celebrity culture, just as her jibes at **Rita Skeeter** are attacks on gossip columnists.

Lockhart, Rowling tells us, is more closely based on a person she knows than any other character in all her books but she doubts the person in question realises this. (Arrogance is another one of this guy's faults!) He mythologises himself in books like **Magical Me**, and appropriates events in other people's lives as his own. A plagiarist par excellence, perhaps he should really have been called Narcissus. But his name is quite appropriate. His heart is 'locked' and he's as showy as gold — or maybe fool's gold. Lockhart was also the name of a Scottish highwayman.

Locomotor Mortis

This is a spell that **Draco Malfoy** uses on **Neville Longbottom** in The Philosopher's Stone to lock his legs together.

Longbottom, Neville

One of the clumsiest characters in Hogwarts, he's always getting into silly situations, but is proficient at herbology. Like **Hagrid**, his idiosyncrasies are amiable. He's a pure-blood. His parents were driven insane by Voldemort's **Death Eaters** when he was just a year old, which gives his character an extra dimension, as well as an extra degree of poignancy to offset the farcical overtones. He's relieved that **Snape** has fled Hogwarts since killing Dumbledore.

Lovegood, Luna

Luna is an eccentric witch who seems to live in her own world a lot of the time, which means that she surprises people when she comes up with bright ideas. She's also prone to foot-in-mouth disease but is attentive to people's sensitivities so is a good egg at heart. Rowling calls her 'my anti-Hermione' character because she's so scatty.

Lovegood, Xenophilius

Luna's eccentric father, who publishes **The Quibbler**. He

appears for the first time in **The Deathly Hallows** but is mentioned in **The Half-Blood Prince**. Xenophilia means 'a love of strange things', as opposed to xenophobia, which means 'suspicion of the unfamiliar'.

Luchian, Sandra

Sandra is a 15-year-old Moldovan girl who couldn't afford to order a copy of **The Half-Blood Prince** from the UK. Since it wasn't on sale in her own country she borrowed a copy from a friend of hers and, wait for it, transcribed the novel in its entirety into five journals. She even wrote the dialogue in black and the narration in blue to distinguish one from the other. It took her a month to get the 607 pages down, but she read it all in two days. That's dedication for you.

Lumos

Charm used to light up the end of a **wand** so it can be used as a flashlight. When you say 'Nox', it 'knocks' off again. Nox is also Latin for night, or darkness.

Lupin, Remus

Professor Lupin is Harry's favourite Defence Against the **Dark Arts** teacher and also a friend and advisor to Harry, but he has demons of his own to negotiate in between lecturing Harry and his colleagues. As a child he was bitten by a werewolf, which gave rise to an incurable condition. His surname derives from the Roman word for wolf, and Lupin himself is indeed a werewolf. His first name is the same as that of the founder of Rome, who was alleged to have been suckled by a wolf as a baby, alongside his brother Romulus.

Lupin is one of Rowling's most interesting and unique characters because when we first meet him, asleep on the Hogwarts **train**, we're inclined to think he's a mole of some sort, a kind of **Peter Pettigrew** or even **Snape** figure. As the books go on, however, we become sympathetic towards him. It takes a good author to make a werewolf sympathetic. Rowling was possibly thinking of her mother's multiple sclerosis when she created him. 'His being a werewolf,' she said in an interview once, 'is really a metaphor for people's reactions to illness and disability.' (He also has to drink a potion every time there's a full moon to stop him from attacking people.) Unlike other animagi in her books he's a reluctant one. He just wants to be Professor Lupin but he finds it difficult to hold down a regular job. (Come to think of it, announcing oneself as a werewolf at an interview for a lectureship might not go down too well.) He dies defending Hogwarts in *The Deathly Hallows*.

Lynch, Evanna

The Irish actress who saw off 15,000 other hopefuls for the role of **Luna Lovegood**. An obsessive Harry Potter fan, she'd been writing to Rowling for years and even made her own ear-rings for the part. 'I *am* Luna,' she told a producer at the casting.

Mackenzie

The name of Rowling's second daughter. She dedicated **The Half-Blood Prince** to her.

Magical Me

The title of **Gilderoy Lockhart**'s autobiography.

Major, John

Not one of Rowling's favourite people. When he was prime minister, he said single parents were a drain on the economy. This was after Rowling's marriage had broken up and she was pulling the devil by the tail financially, having a bad enough time in terms of morale by accepting government assistance without Major rubbing her nose in it.

Malfoy, Draco

Malfoy is French for 'bad faith' and 'draco' Latin for dragon or snake. No wonder Harry's arch-enemy is one of the ringleaders of **Slytherin**. Voldemort tries to get Malfoy to kill Dumbledore but he hasn't the nerve for this, as Dumbledore reminds him shortly before **Snape** kills Dumbledore in *The Half-Blood Prince*. Draco is like a junior Voldemort, probably similar to **Tom Riddle** when he was his age. He goes AWOL from Hogwarts after Dumbledore has been killed.

Malfoy, Lucius

Draco's father. His forename emanates from Lucifer, the devil.

Malfoy, Narcissa

Draco's mother, and Lucius Malfoy's wife. Her forename is the female equivalent of Narcissus, the character from Greek mythology who fell in love with his own reflection. Her egotism expresses itself inversely through the disdain she shows towards others.

Marauder's Map

The magic map Harry uses to get to **Hogsmeade** without being detected. (Professor **McGonagall** has banned him from going there when **Sirius Black** is on the loose.)

Marauders

A group comprising **James Potter**, **Sirius Black**, **Remus Lupin** and **Peter Pettigrew**.

Mathematics

Rowling's worst subject at school. She once scored zero out of ten in a test. (In recent times she's had to improve, just in case the publishers forget a zero after one of her cheques.)

Mayall, Rik

This is the actor who played **Peeves** in *The Philosopher's Stone*. Unfortunately his whole performance ended up on the cutting room floor. (Could we say he disapparated?)

McDonald, Natalie

Natalie was a real person, a nine-year-old girl with an incurable disease. She was an avid fan of Rowling and asked her parents to write to her on her behalf. They did, but she was dead by the time Rowling read the letter. To show her empathy with their grief, Rowling took the unprecedented literary step of actually making Natalie into a student of Hogwarts. So Natalie still lives on the page as well as in the minds of her bereaved.

McGonagall, Minerva

Minerva was the Roman Goddess of Wisdom and this lady, the forbidding Deputy Headmistress at Hogwarts as well as a professor of Transfiguration, exemplifies that characteristic too. At times she appears overly strict but we know there's a core of decency and fair play to her, even when she's reading Harry the Riot Act. Maybe she does this to look good to **Snape**, or perhaps she feels that if she lets her defences down the pupils will play on that. Significantly, she bends the rules by allowing the under-age Harry play on the **Quidditch** team.

Her Scottish origin would have been attractive to Rowling, who is herself partly Scottish. (Hogwarts, of course, is also set in Scotland.) Rowling says she got her surname from the Dundee 'poet' William McGonagall. That's uncharacteristic of her as this gentleman, the generally acknowledged worst author in history, could hardly be regarded as the sharpest knife in the drawer.

McLaggen, Cormac

A name Rowling couldn't resist. He's a conceited – and ruthless – **Quidditch** player who fails to become a Keeper for **Gryffindor**.

Memory

A young boy once quoted the first five pages of *The Philosopher's Stone* to Rowling from memory.

Merchandising

Rowling isn't a great devotee of this practice but she knows it's an occupational hazard of being a cult figure. She keeps a hands-on approach to it to cut down on the tawdry paraphernalia that could (and probably would) accrue in the wake of the global Harry Potter phenomenon. Today the spin-off products, the games, toys and keep-sakes, etc., rake in more money than most people would make in a lifetime. As Anna Whited wrote, 'Books that become classics may inspire film versions, but they don't usually engender hordes of plastic tie-in merchandise, or miniature character collectibles. Imagine Huckleberry Finn's face on a soft drink can, Moby Dick as an action figure sold in discount stores, or a computer game based on Romeo & Juliet.'

Harry Potter isn't just a literary figure now: he's an industry. One writer, Libby Purves, speculated that some time in the future 'Harry is going to get a baby blonde girlfriend and a mid-Atlantic accent. Eventually there will be theme parks with crooked little cute houses down **Diagon Alley**, and games of Virtual **Quidditch** on broomstick roundabouts.' Rowling, who has a certain amount of control over what happens in this regard, says that she will do everything in her power to stop Harry turning up on fast food boxes.

Method acting

Director **Alfonso Cuarón** asked **Rupert Grint** (Ron) to write an essay describing his character during the shooting of *The Prisoner of Azkaban* but he forgot ... because he said that's what Ron would have done.

Millionairess

Rowling was officially declared a millionairess at the end of June 1999. It was something of a shock to the system for a woman who had lived on £70 a week after her marriage broke up.

Mirrors

Mirrors form a central part of fantasy literature, the most obvious example being in **Lewis Carroll**'s *Through the*

Looking Glass, where Alice goes through the mirror in her drawing-room and enters a magical world where everything is back to front. The ancient Greeks believed that mirrors were potent talismans capable, as Allan Kronzeck writes in his book *The Sorcerer's Companion* (Broadway Books) of 'bewitching men's minds, befuddling evil spirits, and carrying off the souls of the living and the dead'.

The most upsetting scene Rowling ever wrote, because it reminded her of the death of her mother, was 'The Mirror of **Erised**' chapter in *The Philosopher's Stone*. ('Erised' is 'mirror' inverted.) Some commentators have written about its similarity to **Tolkien**'s Mirror of Galadriel, and Harry's similarity to Frodo Baggins. (Rowling, like Tolkien and Dickens, if not at least to some extent all children's authors, also relishes making up names that are onomatopoeic.) Dumbledore hides the **Philosopher's Stone** inside the mirror of Erised.

Moaning Myrtle

The ghost who haunts the girls' bathroom at Hogwarts. She was killed by a **Basilisk** that Voldemort released from the Chamber of Secrets but afterwards stayed on at Hogwarts to haunt those who had bullied her while she was alive. She helped Harry during the **Triwizard Tournament** and has afterwards inhabited the boy's toilet to gather information on **Draco Malfoy**'s nefarious schemes for Harry's benefit. She doesn't like to be reminded that she's dead.

Mobiliarbus

Spell used to move a tree without touching it. Mobilicorpus is a similar one used to move a body.

Modus operandi

Rowling used to write in laborious longhand – usually in cafes because there were fewer distractions there – and then transfer the material to her £40 typewriter at night. Thanks to prosperity she can now transfer material more quickly to her computer. (Being the richest children's author in the world, you see, can have its benefits after all.) But she still does her original drafts in longhand and, like all good Luddites, prefers shuffling round with pieces of paper rather than forever looking at a screen. She used to write for up to 10 hours a day but cut back when she became pregnant. Extracurricular activities like promotional work also clashed with her daily workload.

Her favourite writing time is when she's in the middle of a book. That's the most exciting period because she can flex her muscles and play around with concepts and characters. Her worst time is when she's finished. 'At that point,' she says, 'I usually decide what I've written is rubbish.' (We can probably take this last statement, like many of her other ones, with a large dose of something white and crystalline.)

Mollywobbles

Arthur Weasley's pet name for his wife Molly.

Money

No dedicated author writes with this as a primary motivation. At best it's a bonus. No matter how poor Rowling was when her marriage broke up, and she was pretty poor, she still wrote for the love of it rather than any blandishments that could come her way if she hit the top. Sharing Harry with the world (we should remember that she knew him five years before we did) was a sacrifice as well as a delight.

Rowling's books have been estimated as earning over £545 million to date, but this has come at a price. She said once, 'I don't mean to sound ungrateful, but I would gladly give back some of it in exchange for peace and time to write.' (When she missed the Book Awards in 2001, one wag quipped, 'Joanne is away buying a property – Canada.')

Moody, Alastor

This retired Auror is distinguished by his 'mad' magic eye which also has a 'foe glass', enabling him to ferret out his enemies. (The irony is that others should have one of these to ferret him out too.) He turns **Draco Malfoy** into a ferret on one occasion. He comes out of retirement at Dumbledore's request – as **Horace Slughorn** will later do – to become a lecturer in Defence Against the **Dark Arts** (that accursed post nobody succeeds in keeping for long) after Voldemort regains his strength. Before he can begin duties, however, he's attacked by **Barty Crouch** Jr, who goes on to assume his identity. Crouch, as Moody, then tries to kill Harry, but Professor Dumbledore thwarts his plan. Moody is killed by Voldemort in the 'Flight from **Little Whinging**' chapter in *The Deathly Hallows*.

Moore, Roger

This is the name of Rowling's brother-in-law but no relation to the actor who played James Bond. Both he and Rowling's sister Diane showed her much kindness when she was at her lowest ebb both psychologically and financially.

Mosag

Aragog's wife.

Movies

Like many writers, Rowling was weary of any film mogul getting his or her hands on her manuscripts and strangling them out of all recognition on celluloid. But she's been happy with everything **Warner Brothers** has done to date, and indeed with the casts of the movies, with whom she generally keeps in contact to greater or lesser degrees. The films have been as successful as the books from the outset, *The Philosopher's Stone* raking in a cool $900 million to date, which makes it more lucrative even than *Titanic*. *The Philosopher's Stone* cost $126 million to make, which was, relatively speaking, a snip. On the first day alone in the US it took in $31 million. Two days later that figure had risen to $72 million. The first three Harry Potter movies brought in a collective £1.35 billion at the box office.

Muggle-Repelling Charms

These are used at the **Quidditch** World Cup Stadium in *The Goblet of Fire* to keep **Muggles** away. They cause Muggles to suddenly remember a previous engagement and make themselves scarce.

Muggles

Muggles are non-magical people. It's a tribute to Rowling's gifts as a writer that she succeeds in making the **wizards** normal and the Muggles (i.e. the rest of us!) somehow deficient in her upside-down world. It's also a tribute to her that the word Muggle itself has been in the *Oxford Dictionary* since 2003. Of course not all Muggles are dull and unimaginative, like the **Dursley family**. It might be worth mentioning that it took one (Rowling herself) to create non-Muggles. She derived the word from 'mug', just as Dudley Dursley got his name from 'dud', but she also liked the 'cuddly' sound of Muggles. So we're not completely demonised.

Mulciber
A **Death Eater**.

Multiple sclerosis
Rowling's mother died from this at the young age of 45. It wasn't a total surprise because she'd been seriously ill for many years, but it was still a shock and it traumatised Rowling. She expresses some of that trauma vicariously through Harry, who also lost his mother early. 'The Mirror of **Erised**' chapter in *The Philosopher's Stone* was very difficult for her to write from this point of view, but also strangely therapeutic, as if she was working out her grief by working through it on the page.

Mundungus

A stinking tobacco.

Murray, Neil

Rowling married this man, an anaestheologist, in 2001. One of the things that attracted her to him was the fact that he didn't fawn on her, or genuflect in her presence. He said he liked what he read of her first book and they took it from there. In 2003 they had a son, David, and in January 2005 a daughter, **Mackenzie** – a good Scottish name. So now she has three children. (Or four, if we include Harry.)

Nagini

Voldemort's snake, which plays such a large part in **The Deathly Hallows** and confirms him in his Luciferean mode. 'Naga' is Sanskrit for snake. Nagini is beheaded by **Neville Longbottom** in *The Deathly Hallows*.

Names

Rowling says she gets a lot of hers from *Brewer's Dictionary of Phrase and Fable*. Others she makes up out of her head. She thought of the names of the four Hogwarts houses while she was on a plane – and wrote them out on the back of a sick bag so she wouldn't forget them. (Maybe a sick bag is an appropriate place for the word '**Slytherin**').

Nearly Headless Nick

This is the 'nick' name of the quirky, partly decapitated house ghost of **Gryffindor**. His full title is, ahem, Sir Nicholas de Mimsy-Porpington, whose name captures his quirkily aristocratic nature. He harbours an ambition to participate in the Headless Hunt but will probably have to wait a few centuries more before he parts company with his cranium.

Nettleship, John

Nettleship was Rowling's chemistry teacher in secondary school. She wasn't overly fond of him, or indeed his subject, though he claims to have been the person who brought the magical properties of the philosopher's stone to her attention. He was of the old school, which believed that if you spared the rod you spoiled the child. Obviously this wasn't going to work with a shy girl like 'Jo'. After reading her books, however, Mr Nettleship says he has somewhat lost his 'sting'. He also admits he would prefer to have been the template for Dumbledore.

Newell, Mike

Director of the film version of *The Goblet of Fire*, the first time an English person helmed a Harry Potter movie. After it was made he complained that his budget wasn't nearly big enough to get the effects he wanted.

Newton, Nigel

The Chief Executive of **Bloomsbury**. When a decision on *The Philosopher's Stone* was pending, Newton took the manuscript home to read to his eight-year-old daughter Alice. She was charmed by it and he used this as his barometer, wise man. The rest is history – or rather herstory.

Nicolson's

Rowling developed the habit of writing in cafes to escape flats she was sharing with others at a time when she wasn't ready to tell them she hoped to become a full-time writer. Nicolson's in **Edinburgh**, which was run by her afore-mentioned brother-in-law Roger, was her favourite. She used to rock **Jessica** to sleep with one hand and write with the other – a good trick. The environment also seems to have stimulated her. When her circumstances changed she continued the practice, grabbing an hour here and there as Jessica slept and nursing a 'bottomless' cup of coffee to the dregs. (Roger, presumably, kept re-filling it for free and gratis).

The knowledge that her time was limited – Jessica being a light sleeper – seemed to galvanise Rowling, and she spewed out much material in these heated mid-afternoon soirées. (When her daughter awoke it was, 'Goodbye Harry, hello

Jessica'.) Nicolson's is now a Chinese restaurant but tourists still visit it with some enthusiasm, enquiring of the new owners whether this is really where it all began. The street opposite is called, you'd better believe it, Potterrow.

Nigellus, Phineas

The great-great grandfather of **Sirius Black**, and one of Hogwarts' least popular headmasters.

Nimbus 2000

Harry's treasured broomstick, which he uses to great effect at **Quidditch** until it gets whacked to pieces on the **Whomping Willow** after he sees the **Grim** in *The Prisoner of Azkaban*.

Nimbus 2003

An academic conference held in Florida in that year, which is a testament to the growing attention that Rowling's novels were already securing among scholars who had once snubbed their noses at them. Another symposium called 'The Witching Hour' was held in Salem, Massachusetts, in October 2005, an appropriate title and an appropriate place – the scene of witch-hunts in the past.

Norbert

A rare type of Norwegian Ridgeback, this is the baby

dragon that **Hagrid** raises in contravention to the 1709 Warlock law prohibiting dragon-breeding in Britain. Naughty man.

Norris, Mrs

Argus Filch has a cat with this rather unfeline moniker. He uses it as a spy to catch trespassers on his grounds.

Obesity

Dudley **Dursley** suffers from this condition – or should we say enjoys it. Rowling was advised that it was politically incorrect to have an overweight child portrayed in such a negative light, but she persevered nonetheless, her argument being that it was really his parents she was inveighing against for incessantly filling him up with junk food.

Obliviate

To erase parts of a person's memory.

Occlumency

The art of magically defending one's mind against external forces.

Oculus Reparo
This is the spell that Hermione uses in *The Philosopher's Stone* to fix Harry's glasses.

Office work
Rowling says she was useless at this. The only thing she liked about offices, she once confided, 'was being able to type up stories on the computer when no one was looking.' She didn't pay much attention to what was being said at meetings because she was usually 'scribbling bits of my latest stories in the margin of the pad'. This, she admits, is a problem when you're supposed to be taking the minutes of the meeting in question.

Oldman, Gary
Oldman is one of Britain's most accomplished character actors and loves playing villains. He rose to the occasion in fine style to essay the role of **Sirius Black** in the film version of *The Prisoner of Azkaban*.

Ollivander
The man who sells Harry his first **wand**. His name is an anagram for 'An evil Lord'.

Order of the Phoenix

An organisation founded by Dumbledore to combat Voldemort.

Orphan

As an orphan, Harry falls into the Dickensian tradition. He's poorly clothed, shabbily dressed, rarely allowed to speak and generally treated like the lowest form of animal life in **Privet Drive**. The injustice is compounded by the fact that his co-resident Dudley, a total waste of space (and he does occupy quite a lot of it), is so relentlessly pampered.

Owls

Hogwarts uses these rather than carrier pigeons to deliver its mail. When the traditional 'snail mail' fails to alert Harry to his forthcoming mission in the first book (due to Vernon's mean-spirited confiscation of the Hogwarts invitation) a horde of them descend on **Privet Drive**.

In fable, owls were often consulted for their ability to memorise complicated formulas, which may be where the expression 'wise owl' came from. In ancient Egypt they were a symbol of death, but other cultures believe that carrying owl parts around with one conferred special powers. Rowling seems more inclined towards the latter view.

Parallel worlds

One of the distinctive features of the Harry Potter books is the leisurely manner in which the **wizard** and **Muggle** worlds interact and overlap. This is in marked contrast to traditional depictions of fantasy kingdoms like Shangri-La or Oz. Okay, so we can't find Hogwarts on a map, but it's still in Scotland. Neither can Muggles penetrate the wall that leads to **Diagon Alley**, but this is also here. And when Ron is flying in the sky in his **Ford Anglia**, or **Hagrid** on his magic motorbike, they're also in local terrain. **Arthur Weasley**, a pure-blood, enjoys fixing Muggle items (though he can't admit this!) and indeed even praises the London underground at one point for its automatic ticket machines. Elsewhere we see Hermione's Muggle mother happily accompanying her to Diagon Alley for a spot of wizard-shopping. Before Harry realises who he is, he sees many wizards in Muggle-land. He may be marked for glory as the Chosen One, but he also 'does' normal.

One of Rowling's best gifts is her ability to present her wizard world so graphically that we suspend disbelief about it almost immediately. This paves the way for her to do pretty much anything she likes to whomever she wishes without losing her credibility. Such is her expertise in this department that it's almost the Muggles who come across as the abnormal people. Somebody once said that the day after an astronaut landed on the moon, that would spell the end of science fiction, because all we would have left would be science fact. Thanks to people like George Lucas that hasn't happened, and thanks to J K Rowling, fantasy literature is also possible in a world awash with technology. She plays havoc with the space–time continuum in a way that's both funny and inspirational.

Paraphernalia

An innumerable number of games and toys have attended the success of the Harry Potter phenomenon. **Rupert Grint** isn't necessarily pleased by this. 'It's scary to think people are going to be playing with you,' he says.

Parenting

Rowling regards the moment she became a parent for the first time as the greatest one of her life – though getting Harry Potter published was pretty good too. It hasn't been easy trying to change nappies and write books together, as any mother who writes will tell you. 'I've tried my best,' she says, 'but I won't really know how good a parent I've been until my daughter writes "J K Dearest"' – a wry reference to the warts-and-all biography written by Joan Crawford's daughter, which portrayed the screen legend as something of a monster.

The fact that Rowling sets so much store by home life is apparent in her choice of theme for her books. With Harry she's zeroed in on many children's dream: the fact that they're not really the children of their so-called parents. Some children fantasise about being the offspring of royalty. Rowling has gone one better. How many unhappy homes have a neophyte under a metaphorical cupboard waiting for a flock of owls to arrive with a missive from wizard school to pluck them from obscurity?

Parselmouths

These are people who can converse in Parseltongue, i.e. who have the gift of communicating with snakes. Harry proves he can do it in *The Philosopher's Stone* when he expedites the journey of a boa constrictor to Brazil from the local zoo. Voldemort is also a practitioner of it. 'Parselmouth' comes from an Old English word for someone with a hare lip. Harry, of course, has this gift because he's one of Voldemort's **horcruxes**.

Patil, Parvati and Padma

The twins that Harry and Ron bring to the 1994 Yule Ball on a double date that turns out to be a disaster. Many readers detect **sexism** in these pages, as they do in the ones dealing with the Veelas.

Peeves

The mischievous poltergeist who leaves most people feeling rightly 'peeved' when he pulls one of his innumerable stunts, like throwing ink bottles or water balloons on them. Rowling describes him as 'a spirit of chaos'. (She herself owns a cat called Chaos.) As a kind of class clown who delights in making a very noisy nuisance of himself you can't stay mad at him for long – unless you're **Argus Filch**. He's unique in that most poltergeists are invisible but he can be seen – worse luck.

Pensieve

A storage place for memories.

Pensions

Rowling wanted to be a writer from as far back as she could remember but couldn't tell her parents about her dream. They were the type of people, she says, who would have thought, 'Ah yes, that's very nice, dear, but where's the pension plan?'

Peskipiksi Pesternomi

Spell used by **Gilderoy Lockhart** to get rid of destructive Cornish pixies, but it goes wrong, which is hardly unusual for this individual. It was in *The Chamber of Secrets* that Lockhart used this. It's possible he made it up himself.

Pettigrew, Peter

Pettigrew (aka **Wormtail**) was a friend of Harry's father and indeed his Secret-Keeper when **James Potter** was in hiding. He disobeyed the **Fidelius Charm**, however, by revealing the whereabouts of Harry's parents to Voldemort (out of fear for his own life) on the night Voldemort killed them. Pettigrew also helped Voldemort regain his strength after his spell rebounded off Harry, disguising himself as Ron's pet rat Scabbers for 12 years to evade detection and faking his death by cutting off one of his fingers. Harry spares his life at one point, which eventually leads to the death of **Cedric Diggory**, a tragedy for which Harry beats himself up.

Philosopher's Stone

This holds the key to Voldemort's power. It is, of course, the name of the first Harry Potter novel. In the US the book was re-titled *The Sorcerer's Stone*.

Photocopying

In her indigent days Rowling couldn't afford to photocopy pages. At one point she re-typed the entire text of *The Philosopher's Stone* for this reason. Such an exercise enabled her to perform editorial surgery on bits she didn't like.

Pigwidgeon

Ron's owl.

Pince, Madam

The Hogwarts librarian, who runs the library like a prison. This witch is every reader's nightmare, especially if they're noisy or slow to leave at closing time. She evinces a romantic interest in **Argus Filch**.

Platform Nine and Three Quarters

The place where **wizards** go to get out of **Muggle** world by charging through a wall. Some astute commentators have noted its functional similarity to the platform in Eva Ibbotson's novel *The Secret of Platform 13*, which is also the secret entrance to a world of wizardry.

Plotting

Rowling plots her books with near-forensic precision, which means she almost had the denouement of the seventh book worked out before she even put pen to paper for the first. Knowledge of this means that journalists are forever trying to prise confidential information out of her, but they don't get very far. The fact that each book ends at the end of a school year and begins at the beginning of the next gives them a natural pattern that suits her mathematical mind.

Polyjuice potion

This is what **Crabbe** drinks to turn himself into a girl in *The Half-Blood Prince*. It's a drink that can transform one person into another. Hermione suggests to Harry and Ron that they use it to quiz **Draco Malfoy** about his evil plans in *The Chamber of Secrets*. If he doesn't realise who they are, she reasons, he might reveal all.

Pomfrey, Madam

The Hogwarts nurse.

Porto

The Portuguese city where Rowling went to teach English as a foreign language in 1991.

Potions

Asked how she dreams these up, Rowling replied, 'Anywhere and everywhere. Washing dishes, running up the stairs – even on the loo.'

Potter, James

Harry's father, who died when he was a child. Like **Rita Skeeter**, he was an unregistered **Animagus**. What makes him interesting is the fact that he was no angel when he was a student at Hogwarts, though he once saved **Snape**'s life. This made Snape return the favour, albeit grudgingly. (Since then Snape has been the bane of Harry's life.)

Potter, Lily

Lily is Harry's heroic mother, her self-sacrifice acting as a counter-charm to Voldemort's Killing Curse when Harry was a baby. She's always been a keen source of debate among Harry Potter 'anoraks'.

Lily won Harry's protection from Voldemort provided he spent his summers with the **Dursley family** – a convenient way for Rowling to carry on the 'envelope' pattern of most of her books, with their circular plotting.

Potters

The Rowlings lived near a family called the Potters whom Joanne used to play with as a child in her home in Winterbourne near Bristol. They played – need we ask – wizard games. The surname could also have been derived from Beatrix Potter.

Poverty

Rowling hates the romanticisation of the artist who seems to have to be starving in a garret to attain credibility. The reality of her own situation, she often states, is that she was humiliated by poverty rather than enriched by it.

Predictions

In 1996 Rowling was informed by Barry Cunningham, the editor of the Children's Book Division at **Bloomsbury**, that she would never make any money out of kid fiction. Two years later her books were outselling most adult ones by a country mile. Sounds like one of Professor **Trelawney**'s prophecies ...

Pre-existence

Rowling once described Harry Potter as a story waiting for her to find it. Other authors have expressed similar thoughts of their books somehow existing in a separate place before they zoned in on them. A part of her feels it was 'given' to her. In some ways it wrote itself, after she came up with the original concept of a wizard who didn't know he was one until his 11th birthday. From this acorn the oak tree grew. Or should I say the magic mushroom.

Preferences
Rowling once confessed, 'I was happier as an impoverished and unpublished writer than I have ever been as a solvent and mediocre executive.'

Prequel
Rowling denies she'll ever write one of these, unlike George '**Star Wars**' Lucas and his ilk. In other words, when it's over it's over.

Prewett, Fabian and Gideon
Two of **Molly Weasley**'s siblings.

Prewett, Molly
The maiden name of **Molly Weasley**.

Prince, Eileen
Snape's mother.

Priori Incantatem
A reverse spell.

Priori Incantato

This is like a repeat button on a remote control. It makes a **wand** perform its previous spell anew.

Priorities

Rowling once turned down the Queen for her daughter. She was due to receive an Author of the Year award from Her Majesty but took a rain check on it…because she didn't want to miss seeing **Jessica** in a school play that was on at the same time.

Privacy

Being the most famous, if not the richest, children's author on the planet has made Rowling, like most other rich and famous authors, 'row' back her private life. In early interviews she was perhaps over-familiar with journalists. Now she's doubly careful before going into any personal details, for fear of both being misquoted and having facts used against her. It's also impossible for her to answer all her fan mail. If she did there wouldn't be any time left to write the books.

Rowling does as many autograph signings as she can but if there are 1000 children present at a signing and she only gets to 999 of them for one reason or another, she can become maligned as having become too reclusive or too big for her boots or a host of other **Muggle**-like onslaughts. At times she must wish she could don Harry's **Invisibility Cloak** as she tries to sneak out for a quiet espresso without being swamped by fans looking for her to sign some spin-off product from the Harry Potter franchise.

Privet Drive

The **Dursley family** live at this address. Rowling is probably making a reference to privacy. The word also suggests the mediocrity of leafy suburbia. Nobody does anything out of the ordinary here, and people strongly disapprove if they do. (Just the place for a bunch of wizards, owls, flying motorbikes, human cats and what have you.)

Publicity

Rowling says she only reads 'a hundredth' of what's written about her.

Put-Outer

This self-explanatory item is what Dumbledore uses to extinguish the street lights at the beginning of *The Philosopher's Stone*. It is also called a **Deluminator**.

Quaffle

One of the balls used in **Quidditch**.

Quality

Just how good a writer is J K Rowling? Her detractors put her success down to a combination of aggressive marketing and the fact that she was simply in the right place at the right time. These two factors have undoubtedly contributed to her supersonic rise to fame. As we all know, the whole book trade, like most other trades these days, is very much about hype. Also, Rowling fills a gap in the market left by the relative demise of the fantasy/adventure genre with her 'retro' style. There are no DVDs or Game Boys in her books, but she more than makes up for them with her vast array of gadgets. She's also made reading 'trendy' for children again, which can't be a bad thing. (We could cite here the story of the young boy who received a book for a Christmas present from his father some years ago and, after looking at it in disgust for a few moments, enquired 'Where do the batteries go?')

Such considerations apart, Rowling is excellent at building up suspense, not  only within the novels, but also between them. The single caveat one could have about her writing is her continuous prioritisation of planning. Great literature is usually written on the wing, as it were, without a master (or mistress!) plan. Writers will often say things like, 'I didn't know what I wanted to say until I said it.' Rowling, on the contrary, sets a lot of store by a bird's eye view of her works, right down to the fact of knowing how many students were in a particular class on a given day, or what they wore and/or ate. This kind of punctiliousness works a treat for her – apart from creating some obvious chronological headaches at the planning stage – but it would be unwise to issue it as a general edict for prospective scribes. It would strip writing, in particular children's writing, of the spontaneity and serendipity that makes it so thrilling.

Quibbler, The

The magazine edited by **Luna Lovegood**'s father, Xenophilius.

Quidditch

A convoluted combination of rugby, football, cricket, polo, lacrosse and basketball played with broomsticks, this game seems to have intrigued readers almost as much as the more overtly dramatic encounters with horrific creatures in the books. Its popularity seems to slot the Harry Potter books into the **boarding school** genre more than the **wizard** one, except that in the former sport was usually used as a substitute for sexual energy whereas Rowling, at least in the later books, introduces romance into her young characters' lives.

She says she invented the game in a pub one night after an argument with her boyfriend. One imagines her sitting in the pub as a game of soccer, perhaps, was being shown on a TV in another corner, subverting the culture of the time and undermining the laddishness. Rowling may not know much about the offside rule, but when you're subverting hallowed traditions who cares? She's hugely grateful to her boyfriend for arguing with her that night, as well she might be.

Quirrell, Quirenius

This Defence Against the **Dark Arts** professor appears vulnerable to us at first sight (partly on account of his stutter), but his lethal side comes to the fore when we realise he's been brainwashed by Voldemort. The reason he wears a turban on his head is because Voldemort's face is on the back of it. He claims it was given to him by an African prince as a reward when he ridded him of an annoying zombie. Quirrell's name conjures up terms like 'quarrel' and 'querulous', which are guides to his character.

R

RAB

This is the mysterious character who beat both Harry and Dumbledore into the **horcrux** cave.

Rabbits

These are Rowling's favourite pets. At the tender age of six she wrote a book about them, featuring her sister Di falling down a rabbit hole and being fed by them. She then submitted the book to Penguin. So even though she was a shy and retiring child, we can see her self-belief even at this age. In *Alice in Wonderland* Alice fell down a rabbit hole and discovered another world there. It was, as it were, her **Platform Nine and Three Quarters**. Harry's namesake

Beatrix created the character of Peter Rabbit. One wonders whether Rowling chose Harry's surname in her memory.

Radcliffe, Daniel

The quizzical young actor who became famous overnight after landing the coveted role of Harry when the first book became a movie. Though 16 000 hopefuls were screen-tested for the role, Radcliffe was picked out of a theatre audience before even having auditioned. Magic! He had, though, played David Copperfield as a boy in the TV film of that name and was also the tailor's son in *The Tailor of Panama* so he did have some acting experience. He claims he caught the acting bug at the age of five.

Daniel is something of a prankster. While shooting *The Philosopher's Stone* he pinched the mobile phone of **Robbie Coltrane** (**Hagrid**) and translated all the messages into Turkish. (He didn't even use a spell, apparently.) Daniel wasn't a great fan of the Harry Potter books before appearing in the movies but that's all changed now. Perhaps the fact that he's one of the richest people in Britain helps his enthusiasm a tad. Both of his parents are agents so there's no way he's going to be caught out by suspicious small print clauses in his contracts. On the day he was selected, his father had accompanied David

Heyman, the founder of Heyday Films, to the play. It was here that the young Daniel was spotted in the audience.

Ravenclaw
The Hogwarts house that prides itself on its qualities of wit and wisdom.

Ravenclaw, Helena
The daughter of Rowena, aka the **Grey Lady**, and a ghost of **Ravenclaw** House. She steals her mother's diadem.

Ravenclaw, Rowena
One of the four founders of Hogwarts.

Readings
Somebody once defined writing as 'the self-invasion of privacy'. The bashful J K Rowling would agree. She's never enjoyed projecting herself, believing that Harry, Ron, Hermione and all her other creations are well able to speak for themselves, thank you very much. But the nature of the beast means that she has to appear in public … and read. The largest reading she ever gave was in the Toronto Sky Dome (home of the Blue Jays Baseball team), where she appeared in front of over 20 000 people. It was a nerve-wracking experience, just slightly preferable to struggling with a three-headed dog in a Chamber of Secrets.

Re-invention

Time magazine praised Rowling for re-inventing fantasy fiction, 'which was previously stuck in an idealised, pseudo-feudal world where knights and ladies morris-dance to *Greensleeves.*'

Relashio

Spell used to make someone let go of something.

Remembrall

This glass sphere was given to the spectacularly forgetful **Neville Longbottom** by his grandmother. In Harry's first game of **Quidditch**, **Draco Malfoy** throws it in the air but Harry catches it just before it reaches the ground. This makes Professor McGonagall realise just how much of a 'natural' he is at the game.

Reparo

Hermione uses this spell to repair a broken glass in a railway compartment door in *The Goblet of Fire*.

Re-writing

Rowling wrote the first chapter of *The Philosopher's Stone* a record 10 times before she was happy with it. She used her sister Diane as an early barometer. Diane laughed. It

was a good omen, and millions of others have continued
that laughter since.

Rickman, Alan

Rickman, he of the sepulchral voice and portentous grimace,
was an ideal choice to play Professor **Snape** in the
movies. Villains are his forte, his most notable slimy turns
before Harry Potter being as the faux-terrorist in *Die Hard*
and as the Sheriff of Nottingham in *Robin Hood: The Prince
of Thieves*. Like many members of the eventual cast of
Harry Potter he wasn't over the moon about the project
until young people he knew heard about it and more or
less told him his life wouldn't be worth living if he said no.
He thought Bruce Willis was tough until he had to tangle
with his nephews and nieces!

Rictusempra

A spell Harry uses on **Draco Malfoy** in *Chamber of
Secrets* to make him laugh incessantly.

Riddikulus

This is the term that dispels **Boggarts**.

Riddle, Tom Marvolo

This alias of Voldemort is an anagram of the sentence 'I am
Lord Voldemort', so the name itself is a riddle of sorts.

Rockwood, Augustus

Like **Sirius Black**, Rockwood is an escapee from **Azkaban**. He becomes a mole for Voldemort, carrying precious nuggets of information back to him from the bowels of Hogwarts.

Romance

The hormones are raging in the later Harry Potter books. In the third one Harry becomes attracted to **Cho Chang**, and in the fourth he takes **Parvati Patil** to the ball. Lavender kisses Ron in *The Half-Blood Prince* and Hermione becomes jealous, inviting **Cormac McLaggen** to the Christmas party to make him jealous. Harry kisses **Ginny Weasley** in Chapter 24 of the book but by the end they've split up. Duty calls, and there are **horcruxes** to be found…

Rowling, J K

Who she? Joanne Rowling, actually, with the initial for 'Kathleen' added at her publisher's suggestion. She was also advised to use the initials rather than the full name because books about wizards before her arrival on the literary scene were generally male-dominated ventures and the publishers felt young male readers would shy away from her one if she were revealed to be a woman. How wrong can you get? She took it on the chin, though.

'I would have let them call me Enid Snodgrass,' she said, 'as long as they published the book.' (Wouldn't it be fitting to have had Enid Snodgrass as one of the characters in the seventh book?)

Kathleen was the name of her favourite grandmother and she also likes the name Joanne ('Jo' to her friends) though she was teased about Rowling at school, being called everything from 'Rowling Stone' to 'Rowling Pin', so she's not quite as keen on her surname. The 'w' is silent, by the way, so 'Row' sounds like what you do in a boat rather than a fight you get into.

S

St Brutus

St Brutus' Secure Centre for Incurably Criminal Boys is the fictional institution the **Dursley family** invent for Harry to hide the fact that he attends a **wizard** school.

St Mungo's

The Hospital for Magical Maladies and Injuries. **Neville Longbottom**'s parents reside here. So does **Gilderoy Lockhart**, suffering from amnesia after a Memory Spell rebounded on him – but as egotistical as ever.

Sales

There were 45 million copies of Harry

Potter books in print by the year 2000. Three years later that figure had risen to 250 million; 10.8 million copies of **Harry Potter and the Half-Blood Prince** went on sale in July 2005. *The Goblet of Fire* sold 3 million copies in the US within 48 hours of its publication, making it the fastest selling book in history. *The Order of the Phoenix* outdid that, selling 1.8 million copies within 24 hours in 2003, so Rowling actually beat her own record. **The Half-Blood Prince** sold 400 000 copies in Tesco's supermarket alone in the first 24 hours after its publication, which is an average of one copy every 53 seconds. In the UK in total it sold 2 million in 24 hours, with 7 million sales in the US in that timespan.

In 1993 Rowling was on national assistance, struggling desperately to make ends meet as she depended on the kindness of strangers and her sister Diane to keep body and soul together. This is why her real life is often compared to a Cinderella story just as Harry's is. She doesn't like this analogy as she feels it's clichéd and superficial. At the time of writing, i.e. before the sales figures of **The Deathly Hallows** have been tabulated, more than 325 million Harry Potter books have been sold worldwide, in everywhere from Mexico to Mozambique, and the series has been translated into over 60 languages.

Scamander, Newt

This is the pseudonym Rowling chose for her book *Fantastic Beasts and Where to Find Them*.

Scar

The lightning scar on Harry's forehead pains him when trouble is near. In this sense it's a bit like the **Sneakoscope**. It's his parents' legacy to him just as much as the fortune they deposited for him in **Gringotts** Bank. It was left on his face after Voldemort tried to kill him when he was a child.

Scholastic

The name of Rowling's US publisher. Scholastic gave her her first taste of big money after buying the rights to *The Philosopher's Stone* for $105 000 in 1997. They did a first print run of 50,000, quite an increase on the number of copies **Bloomsbury** had run off not too long before.

Scottish Arts Council

This body gave Rowling a grant of £8000 when she was writing *The Philosopher's Stone*, thereby enabling her to give up her teaching job and concentrate on writing full time. (She used a lot of the money to buy herself a computer. Food came second.) As Alison Lurie commented, 'It was her fairy godmother, but she still had trouble getting transportation getting to the ball', before **Bloomsbury** took a gamble on her and reaped rich rewards for their faith.

Scrimgeour, Rufus

The successor to **Cornelius Fudge** as Minister of Magic. Voldemort kills him during the **Death Eaters**' take-over of the Ministry in *The Deathly Hallows*.

Secretarial work

Rowling spent some time at this but her mind was generally elsewhere. When she was doing audio-typing, the manuscript in her typewriter was often a novel-in-progress rather than the report she was being paid to work on! And her ear-plugs didn't have the voice of a boss but the music of Beethoven, which seemed to spark her inspiration.

Security

Fame has meant an increased need for security by Rowling. There's a thin line between admiration and paranoia, and many of her fans have traversed it over the years. In 2002 she had an eight-foot wall built around her home in Edinburgh. CCTV cameras followed. It's not quite of Hogwarts proportions yet but she's getting there. Ideally, the **Rita Skeeters** of the world would need a **Marauder's Map** to track her down. One observer noted, 'It would take a crack SAS team even to ring the doorbell.'

Seekers

The most important players in **Quidditch** as they go after the **Snitch**. Harry is the youngest one in a century.

Seidenfeld, Mark

The lawyer who brought the manuscript of *The Deathly Hallows* to the US for editing. He sat on the book for the whole journey to prevent any unwanted eyes scanning its pages.

Sequel

They say a sequel never equals but Rowling had the seven books planned before she finished the first one so she wasn't flying blind. A lot of the groundwork had been laid for the others at that point, so the five years she spent on *The Philosopher's Stone* bore ample fruit.

Seven

This is a number dear to all **wizards** – and wizard authors. Rowling had seven novels planned for Harry Potter, who completed seven years at Hogwarts. In **Quidditch** there are seven rules, seven players per team and 700 possible fouls one can commit. (Just as well Vinnie Jones doesn't play it.) Of her seventh novel Rowling said: 'It will be the biggest because I want to say a long goodbye. It will be like the Encyclopaedia Britannica.' There was some speculation that **The Deathly Hallows** was going to be launched on 7/7/07, i.e. 7 July 2007, but that Rowling changed her mind because this was the anniversary of the date of the terrorist attacks on London's underground in 2005, so she plumped for 21 July instead.

Sexism

Rowling has often been accused of making her female characters docile and compliant and her male ones  buccaneering and adventurous. This is such a superficial reading of her books that it doesn't even deserve the dignity of an explanation. The character of Hermione, as bright and headstrong as she is, would knock the criticism on the head. So would the fact that Harry also has many vulnerable traits that aren't in the mould of the classic male protagonist. Rowling sometimes complains that she's asked to insert a strong female character into her books 'much as one would ask for a side order of chips'. She makes the point that it would go against the grain of her work to artificially throw in 'a couple of feisty, gorgeous, brilliant-at-Maths and great-at-fixing car girls.' She's resisted such tokenism with a vengeance.

Sherbet Lemon

One of the passwords used to secure entry to Dumbledore's office. All the others are also the names of sweets.

Shrieking Shack

This is where Professor **Lupin** hides out when he's undergoing his lunar changes.

Simpsons, The

It's a sign of anyone's cult status that they're asked to do a voice-over in this show. Rowling had a blast with it in 2003.

Sinistra, Professor

Astronomy lecturer who's appropriately named as she's highly suspicious.

Skeeter, Rita

Hack reporter from the *Daily Prophet*. One imagines Rowling created her to settle some scores with journalists who had in the past, to put it mildly, been over-intrusive with her. Rowling herself denies this. Skeeter is an **Animagus** and turns herself into a beetle to get scoops, just as the paparazzi and members of the journalistic profession seem to be able to melt into the woodwork to garner fly-on-the-wall exposés of their unsuspecting quarries.

Hermione captures Skeeter as one point, which may be wish fulfilment on Rowling's part, after realising she's an illegal Animagus. She agrees to free her if she gives up writing for a year. (How Rowling would relish that deal.) In the US a skeeter is a mosquito, conveying the idea of a bloodsucking parasite. Perhaps Rowling thinks of this species as she does of **Dementors**: draining the life around them like soul vampires. Skeeter redeems herself to an extent after writing a damage limitation article in defence of Harry for *The Quibbler*. She gets some gentle persuasion from **Luna Lovegood**, the editor's daughter.

Slug Club

Horace Slughorn sets this up for his favoured students – Harry, Hermione, **Ginny Weasley**, Melinda Bobbin, Blaise Zabini and **Cormac McLaggen**. He feels they'll make their mark on the world some day and likes to publicise his respect for them at parties only they can attend. (**Draco Malfoy** eat your heart out.)

Slughorn, Horace

This is the portly former Head of **Slytherin**, whom Dumbledore coaxes out of retirement in *The Half-Blood Prince*. Ever since he stopped working he's been hiding from Voldemort in **Muggle** houses, terrified of the **Death Eaters** descending on him. He once taught Harry's mother, whom he admires dearly. He comes back to Hogwarts to teach Potions, becoming Head of Slytherin again after Dumbledore's funeral. At one point in *The Half-Blood Prince* Harry gets Slughorn's memory and, as a result, manages to see Voldemort's past and learn more about **horcruxes**.

Slytherin

The demonic Hogwarts House in which Harry could well have ended up if the **Sorting Hat** had had its way. (But he remained haunted by the fact that it was even a possibility, and Dumbledore only partly allayed his concerns.) Once again the name, compounded of words like 'sly' and 'slither', conveys the sense. In fact the letter 'S' is used for many unsavoury characters in the Harry Potter books, like **Severus Snape**, Scabbers, etc. (The 'H' words, on the contrary, tend to convey virtue – Hermione, **Hagrid**, **Hedwig** and of course Harry himself). The animal symbol of Slytherin is a serpent.

Slytherin, Salazar

One of the four founders of Hogwarts.

Smarties

The first book prize Rowling won. She's now won it three times. It's judged by children, which made it particularly sweet to her, if you'll pardon the pun.

Smith, Dodie

Smith wrote *I Capture the Castle*, one of Rowling's favourite books as a child.

Smith, Maggie

The actress who plays the formidable **Minerva McGonagall**. Smith excelled in the role of another Scottish pedagogue in *The Prime of Miss Jean Brodie* and reprised that talent in the Harry Potter movies, where she also has to try to straddle a balance between authority and empathy. Asked why she took the role she replied, 'I knew it would be my pension.'

Snape, Severus

This Potions professor, the head of **Slytherin**, was named after a village. He shares this in common with many other characters in the books, e.g. Dursley, Crouch, Flitwick, etc. His Christian name sums up his 'severe' character, but could also, as Connie Neal observes in her book *The Gospel According to Harry Potter* (Westminster John Knox Press), allude to the fact that he 'severs' his ties to the Dark Lord.

Snape was once a **Death Eater** and in *The Half-Blood Prince* is revealed as the half-blood prince himself – one of Rowling's mischievous surprises. He's also the person who kills Dumbledore in that book so he won't be on many people's Christmas card list. He does save Harry from **Quirrell**'s curse during the **Quidditch** match early on in the series but this is merely to discharge a debt to Harry's father, who once saved his own life.

We always feel that Snape is on the side of the angels, as it were, and he confirms this view in *The Deathly Hallows* when we learn of his abiding love for Harry's mother Lily. We also learn that he only killed Dumbledore after Dumbledore requested him to, knowing his days were numbered. Snape himself is finally killed by **Nagini**.

Sneakoscope
Contraption that whistles when in the presence of someone two-faced.

Snitch
The most important ball in **Quidditch** as its possession virtually guarantees victory. Dumbledore leaves it to Harry in his will 'as a reminder of the rewards of perseverance and skill'.

Sorting Hat
This decides which of the four houses in Hogwarts students

inhabit. It wavers with Harry after he tries it on, as if **Slytherin** is a possibility. Harry feels it's his 'destiny' to be a Slytherin student, an intriguing term that whets our appetite for incidents like the 'twin duel' escapade with Voldemort, or Harry realising that, like Voldemort, he too can speak Parseltongue. The hat performs a secondary function of being able to sense danger.

Speed

A friend of Rowling's says she types 'at the speed of light'. Considering the length of her books, this seems highly plausible.

Spellman's Syllabary

A book used for translating Runes.

Spielberg, Steven

The famous director once wanted to option the Harry Potter franchise for film, but Rowling objected to his idea of merging two books into one and also his choice of Haley Joel Osment (the star of Spielberg's *Artificial Intelligence: AI*) as Harry. Understandably, she wanted him to be played by a British actor. She also feared the general Americanisation of the books if Spielberg were helming them. One rumour suggested Spielberg wanted to call Hogwarts 'Hogwarts High' and give Harry a blonde cheerleader girlfriend. As Steve Norris, former Head of the British Film Commission, put it, 'That would have been like setting *The Catcher in the Rye* in Liverpool.'

Warner Brothers assured Rowling they would stoutly resist any American influence, but they did need an injection of capital stateside to get the project off the ground. Coca-Cola stumped up $100 000 and Rowling was, well, rolling.

Spinnet, Alicia
A **Gryffindor Chaser**.

Splinching
What happens when half of one's body **teleports** away and leaves the other half behind. Sounds sore.

Spoilers
These were leaks to the plots of the books. Many of them were apocryphal or at least speculative headline-grabbers or website-pondering. Rowling herself didn't provide any but was partial to the odd teasing hint if you caught her in a good mood – particularly if there were no **Rita Skeeters** around.

Sprout, Professor
Harry's aptly named Herbology lecturer. He creates some

controversy when he demands that his students wear earmuffs when working with mandrake plants. Some folk traditions hold that mandrakes do actually shriek so loudly when pulled from the ground that they could actually deafen a person with the noise, or even kill them.

Squibs

These are pure-blood **wizards** who have difficulty performing magic, like **Argus Filch** – which is why he opts for the **Kwikspell** course. Rowling seems to have little respect for wizards who perform magic poorly, **Gilderoy Lockhart** being another example. Or is this mere coincidence?

Stag

The form that Harry's Patronus Charm takes.

Star Wars

Sean Smith, the author of a biography of Rowling, says that the Harry Potter saga reminds him very much of *Star Wars*. 'Voldemort is Darth Vader,' he writes, 'Harry is Luke Skywalker, Hermione is Princess Leia, Ron is Hans Solo and Dumbledore is Obi Wan Kenobi.'

Stereotypes

There are many of these in the Harry Potter series. The cruel stepmother. The secret past. The parents one never saw. The near-death experience. The enchanted forest. The aggressive professor at college. The castle on the hill. The boy with the mission. The demonic villain. The clumsy male friend. The female friend who's a swot. The hero as jock figure. The quest. The continual frustrations. The web of intrigue. The rite of passage of our boy wonder on his 11th birthday, the traditional initiation age in primitive sagas. And so on.

In a lesser writer's hands it would all have amounted to little more than pulp fiction, a kind of occult Billy Bunter, but Rowling's comfort with her twin worlds of **Muggles** and magicians makes the whole somehow greater than the sum of its parts. She annoys some readers by the formulaic sameyness of the books, which generally begin at the **Dursleys**, segue into an episodic adventure at Hogwarts which at some point involves a Voldemort threat which Harry manages to stave off with a little help from his friends, as well as a more exotic sporting challenge, and/or some run-in with a hapless Defence of the **Dark Arts** professor before returning to **Privet Drive** to recharge his batteries before the next year's Michaelmas crisis.

There's no doubt that all the books are plot-driven rather than character-driven and to this extent the things that are happening to the characters are usually more interesting than the characters the things are happening to, but this is par for the course in most fantasy books. Rowling isn't pretentiously poetic and admits that she peels away the layers of her narrative onion bit by bit in each book. Author Edmund Kern once asked (rhetorically) if she represented 'the most recent homogenised manifestation of a bankrupt pop culture'. This is excessively harsh but Rowling is well aware of the plough she's furrowing. It's not a hugely original one, but neither is it fast food. She writes middle-brow fiction for the junior chattering classes and is supremely gifted in that niche.

Stouffer, Nancy

This author, whom the world would never have heard about if it weren't for J K Rowling as her books sold poorly, wrote one called *The Legend of Rah and the Muggles* in 1984, though **Muggles** here were imps rather than non-magical people. Its hero was Larry Potter and he also had black wavy hair and wore round specs. In addition, his mother's name was Lilly (the same as Harry's except for the extra 'l'), and there was another character in it called The Keeper of the Garden, similar to Hagrid as Keeper of the Keys and Grounds in Harry Potter.

Stouffer sued Rowling for plagiarism but the case was

thrown out of court in 2002 after Stouffer was found to have submitted false documents to bolster her case. She also forged sales invoices, adjusted a font and altered an advertisement to make it include a trademark symbol. In the end she was fined $50 000 for trying to pull the wool over the judge's eyes. No doubt the similarities between the books were striking, but they're not substantial details.

Any author stealing names isn't very bright as it's not a creative steal. And we know Rowling is bright. After the trial was over Stouffer claimed she'd received death threats in the course of it, as well as a hornet's nest in the post one day. This is surely a measure of how much she was hated and Rowling loved. Rowling had more than enough money to settle out of court with Stouffer before things got ugly but she chose to confront her head -on because of the cloud it would cast on her creativity. In the end it proved to be a wise choice.

Sunday Times

In 2005 this newspaper estimated Rowling's wealth to be in the region of £500 million. 'I don't ever have to work again if I don't want to,' she says, which is about the biggest understatement since Noah said it looked like rain.

Swearing

Rowling says her editor won't allow her characters to use swear words. She doesn't usually give in to bullying like this but it seems to be a sacred law by now. She finds it difficult because, as she says, 'Ron is definitely a boy who would swear.' She gets around it by the use of dashes – and blushes.

Swing

A nightclub in Porto where Rowling used to trip the light fantastic with her close friends Jill Prewitt and Aine Kiely, the latter a jolly Corkonian. She dedicated *The Prisoner of Azkaban* jointly to them.

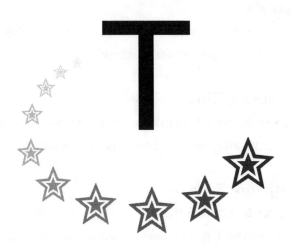

Taboo
The manner of tracing Harry used by Voldemort's followers in **The Deathly Hallows** after Harry has referred to 'You Know Who' by name.

Talisman
What Hogwarts students use to protect themselves from petrification.

Teleporting
Going from point A to B without inhabiting the intervening space. Neat trick.

Thestrals

Fleshless creatures visible only to those who've seen death. In such circumstances, I think I'll pass.

Thicknesse, Pius

Minister of Magic who's under the **Imperius Curse**. He gets the post after **Rufus Scrimgeour** is killed.

Thompson, Emma

Thompson is one of the most gifted – and likeable – actresses in the UK. She was an ideal choice to play the ditsy Professor **Sibyll Trelawney**. 'In one scene in *The Goblet of Fire*', she says, 'I have a nervous breakdown and get to stand at the top of the stairs waving an empty bottle of sherry around the place. This is a fairly typical scene from my daily life so it wasn't much of a stretch.'

She took the part, she says, because if she didn't, her daughter threatened to 'divorce' her.

Three Broomsticks

The main tavern in **Hogsmeade**.

Time-Turner

Hermione receives this device from Professor **McGonagall** to enable her to double up on her classes.

Since the academic day is clearly not long enough for the workaholic Hermione she sees it as a godsend. Both she and Harry later use it for an added purpose – changing the future – when she saves the life of **Buckbeak**.

Speaking more generally, Rowling herself is a 'time-turner' in the sense that she returns literature to its traditional roots. Edmund Kern describes her as a 'retrolutionary', a pun she would enjoy. As regards the specific structure of the books, he points out that each of them moves both backward and forward simultaneously, because the further we travel into Harry's future, the further we also go into his parents' past.

Titles

Rowling has always guarded these obsessively. If any of them had ever leaked out before she or her editor wished, she would have had to change it. If she didn't, she joked that her publisher would have put out a contract on her instead of giving her one! The title of *Harry Potter and the Philosopher's Stone* was changed to *Harry Potter and the Sorcerer's Stone* in the US because the publishers didn't believe it was possible to successfully market a children's book with the word 'Philosopher' in it. Patronising, or what?

Tolkien, J R R

This author was a major influence on Rowling. Those who knew her before she became famous speak of her with her head often buried in a dog-eared copy of *The Lord of the Rings*. Her ex-husband says it was the book she read most often in Portugal. Strangely enough, she had most of her own books written when she got round to reading Tolkien's more accessible *The Hobbit*. She lacks Tolkien's epic sweep and doesn't purport to put herself in the same league as him, but she shares his punctilious planning and plotting.

Tonks, Nymphadora

This lady, half-blood daughter of Andromeda, is a Metamorphmagus, which means she can change her appearance at will, even without **Polyjuice**. She belongs to the **Order of the Phoenix**. She marries **Lupin** but is killed by the **Death Eaters**.

Trains

Rowling's parents met on a train and the idea of Harry Potter also came to her when she was on one so you don't need to be a genius to guess that she likes this particular mode of transport. (Planes are another source of inspiration –

Rowling thought up the names of the four Hogwarts houses on one of these.)

This is how it happened. She was travelling from Manchester to London and the train broke down. The whole magical world of the 'boy who lived' and who didn't know he was a **wizard** until his 11th birthday came to her inexplicably as she gazed through her window at some cows. She saw all her characters in her mind and ached to jot some notes about them down on paper. As luck would have it, none was to be found. Four hours later she finally committed her 'train' of thought to paper, curiously thankful that she had the time to mull over it all in her head, which probably gave it more of a structured format.

Many years later, in 2000, Rowling had a quite different experience on a quite different train. It was a make-believe Hogwarts Express that **Bloomsbury** publishers had constructed to promote *The Goblet of Fire*. The idea was that she would stop at various stations where children would be waiting for her. Rowling herself believed that she would be allowed out at each stop to sign copies of the book but there was no time for that so she had to be content to wave at the hundreds of fans. Many of them cried because they didn't get to meet her, which made her decide she'd never do a promo event of that nature again. It must have been like looking at the mirror of **Erised** for her – so near and yet so far from people she wanted to meet.

Transfiguration

The process of turning one thing into another, as when Professor **McGonagall** turns her desk into a pig to demonstrate the art.

Translations

Rowling's books have been translated into over 60 languages in 200 countries. Sometimes this creates problems. A 'jumper' in Britain is something one wears while in the US it could be somebody leaping from a high-rise to their death, or a pinafore dress. ('Harry has enough problems without going around the place in drag,' Rowling comments drolly.) Rowling drew the line at having Ron's mother referred to as Mom. 'Mrs Weasley is *not* a mom!' she insists. The American versions of the books also change Sellotape to Scotch Tape, thereby losing the pun on Spellotape, which is used to repair **wands**.

Some details in foreign translations have disappointed Rowling. In the Spanish Harry Potter, for instance, **Neville Longbottom**'s toad, **Trevor**, which he's always losing, is translated as 'turtle'. As Rowling points out, 'It's rather more difficult losing a turtle than a toad.' In the Italian translation, Dumbledore becomes Professor 'Silencio'. Here the translator takes the first part of his name out of context, neglecting to note that Dumbledore is an old English word for a bumble bee and that Rowling chose it because her image of the venerable professor was of a man 'always on the move, humming to himself'.

Travers

A **Death Eater**.

Trelawney, Sibyll

Harry's Divination professor. A doomsday prophetess of sorts, in *The Prisoner of Azkaban* she predicts death for him when she sees the image of a **Grim** – a portent of the Grim Reaper – in his tea leaves. In her palmistry lessons she tells him he has the shortest life line she's ever seen.

In Greek mythology Sibylla was a seer, and much more reliable than Ms Trelawney in her predictions. The latter starts off well, impressing Dumbledore by telling him a child will be born that will threaten Voldemort but since then her radar has been on the blink and her prophecies very much hit-and-miss affairs – no more reliable than **Rita Skeeter**'s Daily Prophecies. 'Tripe, Sibyll?,' Professor **McGonagall** asks her during a Christmas dinner in *The*

Prisoner of Azkaban, Rowling having fun with one of her familiar puns.

Sibyll sometimes goes into trances when making her predictions. She also has a drink problem. She's dismissed from Hogwarts by **Dolores Umbridge** but subsequently reinstated.

Trevor

Neville Longbottom's pet toad, which he's forever losing. It was given to him by his great-uncle Algie as a reward for having miraculously survived a fall from a window as a child. (Algie dropped Neville after being distracted by some meringues.) In ancient times toads were rumoured to play a central role in the initiation ceremonies of new witches.

Triwizard Tournament

A competition between the three main wizarding schools in Europe that consists of three main tasks: to get through a maze, to get past a dragon and to rescue a hostage from under a lake. Each school is only supposed to have one entrant but Hogwarts enters both Harry and **Cedric Diggory**, making it more into a 'Quadwizard' event. This makes Harry unpopular (even Dumbledore sees him as a glory-seeker for a while) but it wasn't his decision. His name was entered without his knowledge. He's allowed to compete even though he's under age because his name comes out of the **Goblet of Fire** in the book of that name. **Rita Skeeter**, needless to say, hovers around all of this, sniffing a hot scoop.

Trotter, Barry
Michael Gerber's name for the Harry Potter spoof series. We could compare it to A R R R Roberts' spoof on *The Hobbit*, which he calls *The Soddit*, or his parody of *The Da Vinci Code*, called *The Va Dinci Cod*. Roberts called another one of his books *The Sellamillion* so he's not shy about setting out his mercenary stall.

Twain, Mark
In some ways we can see Harry as similar to Twain's most famous character, Huckleberry Finn, who also escapes from dull domesticity for the Great Outdoors.

Twelve Angry Men
This courtroom drama is **Daniel Radcliffe**'s favourite black and white film.

Twycross, Wilkie
Apparition instructor who appears in *The Half-Blood Prince*.

Umbridge, Dolores

This professor, who lectures on Defence Against the **Dark Arts**, licks up to **Cornelius Fudge** in *The Order of the Phoenix* to climb up the Hogwarts ladder. She subsequently usurps Dumbledore's position as chief wizard. Harry falls foul of her, as does **Hagrid**, when she starts to rule with an iron fist. At one point she even sends the **Dementors** after Harry to prise information out of him. Her first name probably derives from 'dolor', the Latin word for pain. Her surname signifies the fact that she's continually taking 'umbrage' on flimsy pretexts.

Unforgivable Curses

There are three of these: **Avada Kedavra**, which causes instant death; **Imperius**, which gives the source total control over his/her prey, virtually brainwashing them; and **Cruciatus**, which inflicts horrific pain.

Unicorn

Voldemort drinks the blood of this fabled creature with the horn on its forehead to gain strength.

Uranus

One of Rowling's naughtier puns. Go figure.

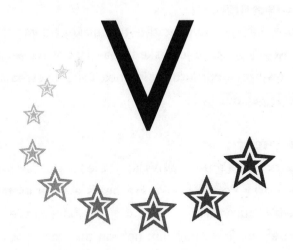

Vane, Ronilda

The lady who tries to make Harry drink a love potion, à la **Merope Gaunt,** in *The Half-Blood Prince*. (Ron accidentally drinks it afterwards.)

Vault 713

The one used to hide the **Philosopher's Stone**.

Vector, Professor

Hermione's **Arithmancy** lecturer. Rowling – as ever – uses an apt term for his name, vector being a mathematical term.

Veritaserum

A potion like sodium pentathol that makes people tell the truth. Rowling was once asked in an interview what she would divulge about future plotlines if she ingested it. The answer? Precious little.

Voldemort

This Dark Lord (You-Know-Who) is the Faustian arch-villain of the Harry Potter books. He bears a resemblance to **Tolkien**'s Sauron from *The Lord of the Rings* in the sense that when we first meet him he's on the way back to full strength after a period of weakness. His name literally stands for 'flight from death'. He wants to cheat death like the **Flamels** and is prepared to go to any lengths to do so. He also wants to take over the world, like every arch-villain from ancient times to the Darth Vader of *Star Wars*. The fact that he's 'offstage' for most of the books increases his aura of danger. Unseen enemies somehow always seem worse. On the other hand, the repeated mention of him as 'He-Who-Must-Not-Be-Named' loses its effect over time, becoming more coy than ominous.

Voldemort is the son of a witch and a **Muggle**. His mother didn't tell her husband she was a witch until she became pregnant. When she did, he flew into a rage and left home. Voldemort, whose name then was **Tom Marvolo**

Riddle, grew up in a Muggle orphanage. He never forgave his father for deserting him. He started practising wizardry at Hogwarts at the age of 11 and shortly afterwards began his killing career, collecting disciples around him that he called **Death Eaters**. He killed his father and also his father's parents before waging an all-out war against Muggles, and even Muggle-friendly **wizards**.

When Harry was a baby, as mentioned before, Voldemort put a killing spell on him but the spell rebounded on Voldemort himself, thereby weakening his powers. Many of the Death Eaters were arrested and imprisoned at this time. Voldemort managed to stay alive by inhabiting the bodies of animals. He dies when The Killing Curse reverses on him in *The Deathly Hallows*.

Waddiwasi

A spell used by Professor **Lupin** that makes chewing gum go up **Peeves'** nose to punish him for putting it in a keyhole.

Walters, Julie

The actress who plays **Molly Weasley**. She wasn't familiar  with the Harry Potter books before being offered the part in *The Philosopher's Stone* but her daughter Maisie soon 'educated' her. Her down-to-earth nature is ideal for Molly. As **Christopher Columbus**, who directed her, remarked, 'She treats everyone the same, from the cleaners to me.' She also improvised lines delightfully, as in the scene where Ginny asks her if she knows where her jumper is and she replies casually, 'Yes, dear, it's on the cat.'

Wands

The use of wands in the Harry Potter books is as effective as swords in swashbucklers or guns in cowboy films. Hundreds of fans send them to Rowling and she gives them all to her daughter **Jessica**. If Jessica ever decides she wants to be a witch, she'll hardly have to buy one from Mr **Ollivander**.

Wand writing

A form of writing in air that Dumbledore employs in *The Philosopher's Stone*, using ribbons from his **wand**.

Warner Brothers

Rowling sold the rights to her books to this film studio in 1998 for $500 000. They got them cheaply as things worked out.

Watson, Emma

This cute actress adeptly captures both the precociousness and charm of Hermione in all the movies, though some readers have justifiably complained that she's much more glamorous than the 'plain' Hermione described in the books. (This is one of Rowling's few concessions to the dictates of commercial cinema.) She's bright as a button and sharp as a tack but also carries the emotional fragility of her character, albeit under wraps. Asked what she would do if she really possessed magic powers, she replied, 'I would get Brad Pitt to appear in one of the films with me.' I'm sure Angelina Jolie would have something to say about that. Either way Messrs Radcliffe and Grint had better watch out.

Waugh, Auberon

Waugh was perhaps an unlikely apologist for Rowling, who might be construed as writing lowbrow fiction in his eyes. He commended her for 'saving a generation from total illiteracy' – a reference to the fact that children who never read books before she came along suddenly felt undressed without one in their schoolbag or bedside locker.

Weasley, Arthur

Ron's father. Though a pure-blood himself, he likes **Muggles** and objects in the Muggle world, which he takes great delight in repairing in the Misuse of Muggles Artifacts Office where he works. (His fondness for 'Muggle stuff', however, has worked against his chances of promotion.) He's like a surrogate father to Harry, who enjoys his homespun ways, and helps him escape from the **Dursley family** in his **Ford Anglia** after he misses the Hogwarts Express. Money doesn't seem to matter much to Arthur, which is probably why he's never had much of it. His family have to make do with little, poor old Ron even having to work with a hand-me-down **wand** when we first meet him.

Weasley, Fred and George

These identical twins were born on April Fool's Day and live life as if it were an extension of that. They're always up to some mischief or other but perform helpful actions too, as when they steal the **Marauder's Map** from **Snape**'s office and give it to Harry to help him get to **Hogsmeade** without being detected. They make something of an ignominious exit from Hogwarts after **Dolores Umbridge** becomes Headmistress, but go on to fulfil their collective life's dream of running a thriving concern at **Diagon Alley** with their Weasley's Wizard Wheezes Shop, Harry kindly stumping up the investment cash for same from his earnings at the **Triwizard Tournament**.

Weasley, Ginny

Ginny's innocent use of Voldemort's magic diary leaves her open to exploitation by him. She's captured by **Tom Riddle** and imprisoned in the Chamber of Secrets but rescued by Harry. She's had a crush on Harry from Book

One but they don't become official girl – and boyfriend until *The Half-Blood Prince*. Even then, Harry's attention is diverted by the knowledge that he will soon have to engage Voldemort in a do-or-die combat. (Priorities, priorities.) He finally kisses her in Chapter 24 of *The Half-Blood Prince*, and, in the epilogue of *The Deathly Hallows*, we learn that he later marries her. They have three children, named James, Lily and Albus Severus after Harry's parents, Dumbledore and **Snape**.

Weasley, Molly

Arthur's wife, who has her work cut out for her trying to manage her seven children, especially the terrible twins **Fred and George**. She also knits, but badly, and people fear her sartorial creations. She has an uncharacteristic crush on **Gilderoy Lockhart**.

Weasley, Percy

The most unlikeable member of the Weasley family, this not-so-perfect prefect is ruthlessly ambitious. He has little loyalty to anyone as he pursues his aim to become Minister of Magic. He's a necessary addition to the Weasleys as most families have at least one rotten apple in the barrel, and if he weren't in the books the family would probably have been regarded as being too idealised. He redeems himself in *The Deathly Hallows* by resigning from the Ministry of Magic and fighting with Dumbledore's Army at the Battle of Hogwarts.

Weasley, Ron

Harry's best friend, showing true grit in times of crisis even if his methods are unorthodox. Rowling modelled him on her childhood friend Seán Harris. If Harry is Oliver Twist, Ron is the Artful Dodger.

Websites

There are reputed to be over a million websites relating to the Harry Potter books in some shape or form. The official one is www.jkrowling.com.

Whisp, Kennilworthy

This is the quirky pseudonym Rowling chose for her book *Quidditch Through the Ages*.

Whitbread Award

Rowling won this in 1999 and was nominated again in 2000 but lost out to Seamus Heaney for his translation of the extended Òlde English poem 'Beowulf'. She did, however, win the Children's Whitbread award that year, and wasn't at all ashamed to play second fiddle to the Irish Nobel Prize Winner.

Whomping Willow

This tree can attack people. It isn't one of Harry's favourites as it destroys the **Ford Anglia** in which he's escaping from the **Dursleys** in *The Chamber of Secrets*, and also his **Nimbus 2000** during a game of **Quidditch** in *The Prisoner of Azkaban*.

Williams, Robin

This actor is so keen to appear in a Harry Potter movie he says he'd do it for nothing. So far neither **Warner Brothers** nor Rowling is biting, surprisingly enough.

Wind in the Willows

Rowling's father read this to her when she was suffering from measles at the age of four. It gave her her first love of reading.

Winder, Rob

Winder is famously (or rather infamously) critical of the Harry Potter books and he didn't mince his words with the last one either, claiming it lacked 'the surreal fun of Dahl, the epic fantasy of Tolkien and the seething tension of Susan Cooper'. He finished his review by saying that Harry was like a fast-food French fry: 'a triumph of marketing over genuine content', but then added with as much tongue in cheek as he could muster, 'Of course French fries are enjoyed by people all over the world. They can't all be wrong, can they?'

Wingardium Leviosa
A levitating charm.

Winky
House elf that used to serve the Crouch family before getting her marching papers from **Barty Crouch** after he finds her with a **wand** that once conjured up the **Dark Mark**. She hates her freedom, having been conditioned to servitude for so long, and takes to drink to drown her sorrows when she gets it. She's particularly partial to butterbeer, a drink only elves can get drunk on. **Dobby** frequently nurses her back to health after her bouts of drinking.

Witherwings
Another name given to **Buckbeak**.

Wizards
Rowling believes there are about 3000 of these in Britain at the moment.

Wormtail
The nickname of **Peter Pettigrew**, who turns himself

into Ron's pet rat Scabbers. Pettigrew cuts off his finger at one point to help Voldemort's return to power. When he turns into a rat, the rat is missing a toe. Rowling got the name from her sister Diane's fear of rats – especially their tails. He finally redeems himself in **The Deathly Hallows** by sparing Harry's life, but pays for this gesture with his own, Voldemort causing him to strangle himself by his own artificial hand – which has been made by Voldemort.

Wright, Cliff

Wright illustrated the covers of the second and third Harry Potter books.

Writer's block

Rowling hasn't suffered from this very much but while she was writing *The Goblet of Fire* she became so frustrated she fantasised about breaking an arm to enable her to push back her deadline date with her publishers. She also had writer's block to a degree during the composition of *The Chamber of Secrets*. *The Philosopher's Stone*, its predecessor, had been such a runaway success she was worried she mightn't be able to emulate it – a groundless fear as things worked out – and froze from panic for a while as a result of what's generally referred to as 'The Second Book Syndrome'.

There was a rumour she also had it while writing *The Order of the Phoenix*, a book that missed its original deadline by some margin, but we should remember that while she was writing this the legal action of **Nancy Stouffer** was hanging over her head. Anybody would find it difficult to concentrate on a fantasy world with that reality check hovering.

The critics have generally been kind to Rowling but no writer has an endless honeymoon and as the books have gone on and grown more bulky, more critics have come out of the closet. They've accused her of lowering the standards that made the first book so exciting as quantity varied inversely with quality in their view.

XYZ

Yaxley

The Ministry official who appears at the beginning of **The Deathly Hallows** to tell Voldemort when Harry will reach 17 and finally depart the **Dursley family** for good, thereby leaving him susceptible to being killed by Voldemort.

Yemets, Dmitri

Russian author who unashamedly plagiarised Rowling in his novel *Tanya Grotter and the Magical Double Bass*, a title which almost in itself gives the game away. He was brought to court by her lawyers just before he finished a sequel, *Tanya Grotter and the Disappearing Floor*. Yemets claimed he was parodying Rowling rather than plagiarising her but the judge didn't buy it.

Yolen, Jane

Yolen wrote a book called *Wizard's Hall* in 1991. It centres on an 11-year-old character called Henry who, after being called to wizardry school at that age (the same as Harry Potter), discovers that he too is special, being the 113th pupil. This means that he has the power to undo a curse put on the school.

As author Connie Ann Kirk has observed in her biography of Rowling, Henry also thinks about his dead mother a lot, like Harry, and the bedroom ceiling in Henry's room is open to the sky in the same way as the ceiling of the Great Hall in Hogwarts in the Harry Potter books. Further, Henry and his friends – not going by the names of Ron and Hermione but showing some resemblances to them – glean much of their wizard-oriented information about grisly goings-on from the school library and by wandering about the place after dark when all their fellow students are a-bed.

Yolen never accused Rowling of plagiarism, as Nancy Stouffer did, Kirk deducing that there's a professionalism among successful authors (Yolen has over 200 books to her credit) that accepts a thematic crossover that's either unconscious or coincidental or a bit of both. Rowling was a voracious reader in her childhood and it's likely she soaked up the influences of more authors than she herself even remembers in pursuit of her own vision.

Zonkos
The joke and gift shop in **Hogsmeade**.